Calgary's Union Cemetery

A Walking Guide

Harry M. Sanders

FIFTH
HOUSE

Design by John Luckhurst / GDL
Cover photographs by Michael Interisano, Mirror Image Photography
Original interior photographs by Shannon Lee Rae
Illustrations by Lori Andrews
All scans by St. Solo Computer Graphics Inc.

The publisher gratefully acknowledges the support of The Canada Council for the Arts
and the Department of Canadian Heritage. We acknowledge the financial support of the
Government of Canada through the Book Publishing Industry Development Program
for our publishing activities.

Printed in Canada by Friesens.

02 03 04 05 06 / 5 4 3 2 1

NATIONAL LIBRARY OF CANADA CATALOGUING IN PUBLICATION DATA

Sanders, Harry Max, 1966-
  Calgary's historic Union Cemetery

  Includes bibliographical references.
  ISBN 1-894004-56-6

  1. Union Cemetery (Calgary, Alta.)—Guidebooks. 2. Calgary
(Alta.)—Biography. 3. Calgary (Alta.)—History—Anecdotes. I.
Title.
FC3697.61.S26 2002   929'.5'09712338   C2001-911704-3
F1079.5.C35S26 2002

Fifth House Ltd.
A Fitzhenry & Whiteside Company
1511-1800 4 St. SW
Calgary, Alberta, Canada
T2S 2S5

1-800-387-9776
www.fitzhenry.ca

TABLE OF CONTENTS

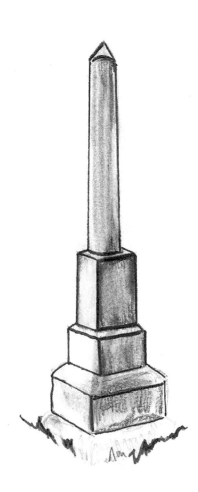

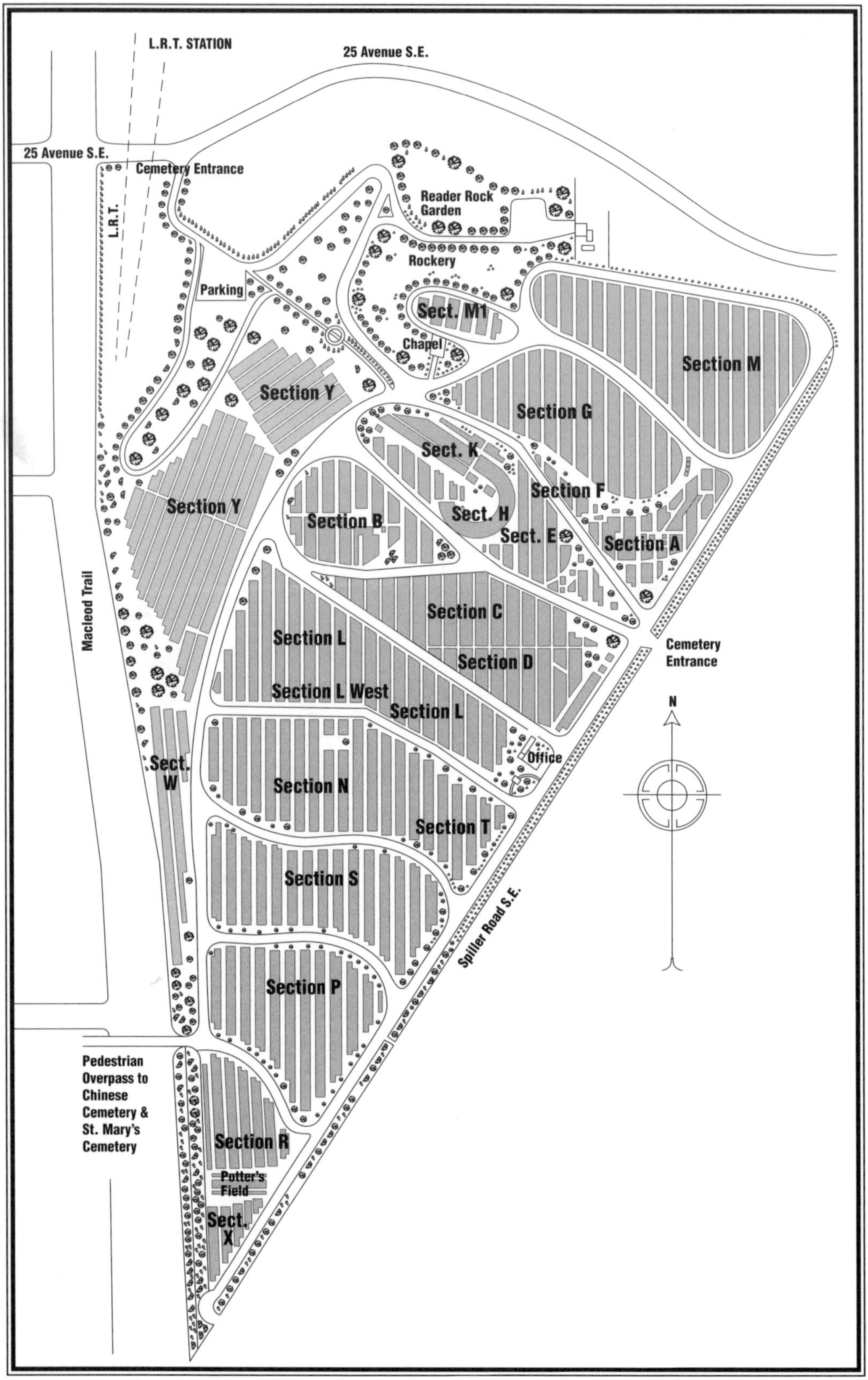
L.R.T. STATION
25 Avenue S.E.
25 Avenue S.E.
Cemetery Entrance
Reader Rock Garden
L.R.T.
Rockery
Parking
Sect. M1
Chapel
Section M
Section Y
Section G
Sect. K
Section F
Section Y
Sect. H
Section B
Sect. E
Section A
Section C
Macleod Trail
Section L
Cemetery Entrance
Section D
Section L West
Section L
N
Office
Sect. W
Section N
Section T
Section S
Spiller Road S.E.
Section P
Pedestrian Overpass to Chinese Cemetery & St. Mary's Cemetery
Section R
Potter's Field
Sect. X

ACKNOWLEDGEMENTS

In writing history, one is constantly reminded of the old maxim about standing on the shoulders of giants. I am deeply indebted to the works of Calgary historians past and present, including David Bright, Hugh Dempsey, James H. Gray, Max Foran, Donna Mae Humber, Henry Klassen, Grant MacEwan, Leishman MacNeill, Jack Peach, and Donald B. Smith. No work of Calgary history would be worth researching or writing without the enormous help of the librarians and archivists at the Calgary Public Library, City of Calgary Archives, Glenbow-Alberta Institute, Legal Archives Society of Alberta, and the University of Calgary Archives. Several fellow historians and enthusiasts shared their research generously with me and offered excellent comments and criticism. Particular thanks go to Jennifer Bobrovitz, Jim Bowman, Kathy Brown, Hugh Dempsey, Rob Graham, Frederick Hunter, Henry Klassen, David Mittelstadt, Lindsay Moir, Judii Rempel, Miriam Sanders, Don Smith, and Don Sucha. Central Parks and Cemeteries Division Manager Archie Lang and his employees provided outstanding assistance, and I particularly wish to thank Cemetery Foreman Joe Blunden for sharing his insights and helping me to find many obscure, unmarked graves. Union Cemetery Foreman Bob Smid was also helpful in finding graves. Roger Hall of Somerville Memorials Ltd. spent many hours with me identifying monument types and materials, and Kelly Taylor and Alias Sanders walked throughout the cemetery with me identifying types of stone. I wish to thank Lori Andrews for providing the line drawings and Shannon Lee Rae for original photography. Thanks are also due to the *Calgary Sun*, where the biographical sketch of Bob Edwards was originally published, to John Adams, whose *Historic Guide to Ross Bay Cemetery* (Victoria: Sono Nis Press, 1998) provided the inspiration for this volume, and to Catherine Radimer of Fifth House Ltd. for recommending me for this project. Most of all, I wish to thank my lovely wife, Kirsten Olson, for her unfailing encouragement and support.

Horizontal column

Bronze pillow

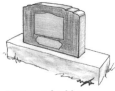

Horizontal tablet
with rounded checks

Western slant

Sepulchral sarcophagus

Vertical tablet with
serpentine top

Rockshell tablet

Flat marker
(flush grass marker)

Veterans' tablets

Vertical tablet with
double pediment

Vertical tablet
with pediment

Vertical tablet
with apex top

Sculptured
scroll pedestal

Sculptured pedestal,
two lambs

Vertical monolithic
tablet

Vertical tablet
with sculptured
top

Free-standing
pedestal

Pedestal with
bead moulding
and ball top

Celtic cross

Free-standing
column with
urn

Pedestal
monument

Free-standing,
broken column

Vertical obelisk

A Heritage Carved in Stone

Calgary's Union Cemetery is a museum, history book, and road map rolled into one. Situated on a landscaped hill only minutes from downtown, this Victorian graveyard is Calgary's oldest existing public burial ground.[1] Though established as a Protestant graveyard, Union Cemetery's interdenominational character is reflected in its name. Among its estimated fifty to sixty thousand "permanent residents" are names instantly recognizable from Calgary's history, many memorialized in streets, parks, and facilities across the city. Through the graves of the rich and the poor, the famous and the unknown, Union Cemetery evokes every theme from the city's storied past.

HISTORY

The history of the City of Calgary began with the 1875 arrival of the North-West Mounted Police (NWMP). A Roman Catholic mission, Our Lady of Peace, had already been established in the area, following on the heels of Roman Catholic missionaries who had previously settled in the district. In time, both the NWMP's Fort Calgary and the Catholic mission to the south attracted further settlement; the fort became the nucleus of Calgary, while the mission developed into Rouleauville, a village later annexed to Calgary and renamed the Mission district.

In 1876, Catholic missionaries established Calgary's first cemetery near what is now 24th Avenue SW, just south of the former Holy Cross Hospital. For nearly a decade there was no corresponding Protestant graveyard, and on occasion non-Catholics—including mounted police officers—were buried in the Catholic graveyard. The absence of a Protestant cemetery was not a serious problem as long as the settler population around Fort Calgary remained low. That situation changed when the still-unfinished Canadian Pacific Railway (CPR) reached Calgary in August 1883. Two weeks later the *Calgary Herald* made its debut, and its pages documented the daily life of the young community.

Less than a month after its first issue, the *Herald* reported that a railway section man named Morrison had died and was buried "beside one of the bluffs, in close proximity to the track."[2] The *Herald* quickly seized upon the incident and editorialized:

> In view of the death which occurred in our town last week, would it not be well to look about and select a spot where the dead may be buried? Our Catholic friends have a burying place at their mission, and two of the constables of the police force are buried there; but as we are all aware, they do not wish to have persons outside the pale of their own Church interred in their grounds, while other denominations are equally desirous of using their own. We think a beautiful site might be procured somewhere on the banks of the Elbow, and enclosed; then at a future time, when our town is located, it can be adorned according as the tastes of the people dictate.[3]

Through the Church's generosity, Protestants continued to be buried in the Catholic cemetery—presumably in an unsanctified area—among them Calgary's first murder victim, James Adams, in February 1884. Once the Town of Calgary was proclaimed in November 1884, one of the first priorities of the new town council was to secure land from the Dominion government for cemetery purposes. Ottawa set aside land at Shaganappi Point, an area west of Calgary on the south bank of the Bow River. The first burials began in 1885, and there over the next half-dozen years some seventy-five bodies were interred. But its distance from the town and its rocky soil made Shaganappi a poor choice, and by 1888 citizens clamoured for a new burial ground.

In the spring of 1890, Mayor James D. Lafferty and three town councillors formed a committee to choose a suitable location. South of the town limits, across the Elbow River, they found what they were looking for: the gently sloping hillside farm of Augustus Carney. After sinking test pits to determine subsurface conditions, council entered an agreement with Carney to purchase sixty-five acres of his Macleod Trail property at seventy dollars per acre. At the time, some thought the property too large for Calgary's needs.

"Rusty" Carney was a notable figure in frontier Calgary. Born in Dungarvan, County Waterford, Carney left his native Ireland in 1847 at the age of five and immigrated with his family to Ottawa, Ontario. In 1881, Carney and his wife Ann moved to the frontier west, and homesteaded on the future Union Cemetery site. In 1884 he became the founding president of the Calgary and District Agricultural Society, forerunner of the Calgary Exhibition and Stampede. He served on the reception committee for the 1886 visit of Prime Minister Sir John A. Macdonald, and had once applied for the position of town scavenger. Augustus's agreement with the Town allowed him to remain in his farmhouse for two more years and to continue harvesting his crops. He was to look after closing the gates, monitor the condition of the fence,

Irish-born Augustus Carney (1842–1923) home-steaded on the future site of Union Cemetery. He later moved to British Columbia and became a police magistrate and timber inspector. Carney and his wife Ann are buried in Kaslo, British Columbia. (Glenbow Archives, NA-1075-27)

and to allow interments only as instructed by council or the town engineer. The Carneys vacated the property in 1892, but bought back a small portion in 1894 to bury their son Alfred (see p. 7).

Although the Calgary Cemetery (as Union Cemetery was first known) had not yet been planned or laid out, council set aside a certain portion at the southwest corner for immediate use. The first official burial was that of Reverend Angus Robertson, Calgary's original Presbyterian minister, in September 1890 (see p. 30). Town council commissioned a contour survey in April 1891, and later that year a plan designed by town engineers Child and Wilson was adopted. To encourage citizens to move their loved ones from the old graveyard, council offered free grave lots and burials at Union Cemetery throughout the summer of 1892. The Shaganappi cemetery was abandoned, although bodies continued to be removed and reinterred at

Union as late as 1911. Some graves whose relocation is unaccounted for might still remain there. The former graveyard became Shaganappi Golf Course around 1915.

Former town constable Robert L. Barker, a veteran of the Northwest Rebellion of 1885, became the caretaker of Union Cemetery in 1892 and moved into the old Carney homestead house. He earned thirty dollars per month, as well as a 10 percent commission for collecting arrears. Before long, he also became responsible for the nuisance grounds ("the dump," in latter-day parlance), which were located just north of the graveyard. In 1899, James H. Galloway assumed the care-taker position. Over the next thirty-four years, Galloway interred some twelve thou-sand bodies—all in hand-dug graves. Both men were later buried in Union Cemetery. The town also engaged a ferryman to provide passage between Calgary and the cemetery. Until the Elbow River was bridged at that point in 1905, funeral par-ties halted at the riverbank; mourners had to wait for the ferry, and could cross only a few at a time.

Before tree planting began in 1899, Union Cemetery remained much as it had been in Carney's time: a windswept, barren hill. In a 1902 petition for cemetery improvements, a large group of prominent signatories vented their frustration: "It is our opinion that a well kept cemetery should be a matter of pride to the city, and not a desolate and almost treeless place such as our cemetery has always been."[4] The City had already made some improve-ments, including a windmill-driven water pump constructed in 1899. The old Carney house was demolished that year, replaced by a brick caretaker's cottage at the ceme-tery entrance along the original Macleod Trail (now Spiller Road). Later covered in stucco, the cottage still stands and is used as the cemetery office, workshop, and garage.

A mortuary chapel, built in 1908, eased the problem of winter burials in an era when graves had to be dug by hand. Graveside services could now be held in the chapel, after which the casket would be lowered through an opening in the floor to the crypts below. The actual burial took place the following spring, after the ground had thawed. (A two-dollar fee was levied if the body remained in the crypts past May 1.) By the 1950s, the introduction of mechanical equipment to dig graves elimi-nated the problem of winter burial, and the mortuary chapel was no longer needed. It has since been used for equipment storage.

The beautification of Union Cemetery began in earnest during Calgary's phenom-enal pre-World War I boom. The city's pop-ulation grew tenfold in a decade, from about four thousand in 1901 to over forty thousand in 1911. The city limits pushed outward, taking in surrounding farmlands, neighbouring villages, and—in 1907— Union Cemetery. The new Victoria Road

Seen from the main entrance, Union Cemetery still appeared barren in 1912. The office to the right has been demolished, but the hilltop mortuary in the background still stands. (Glenbow Archives, PD-117-5)

In its original 1912 location at the cemetery's northwest corner, this neoclassical arch served as a gateway for people entering from what is now Macleod Trail. It was moved in the 1980s. (Glenbow Archives, PD-117-13)

(now part of Macleod Trail) was built over Cemetery Hill, forming Union Cemetery's western boundary. Across that road lay the private Jewish and Chinese cemeteries, separated from Union in 1904 and 1908 respectively. By 1912 the streetcar reached the cemetery gates.

One of the new civic professionals hired during the boom was Richard Iwersen, parks superintendent from 1911 to 1913. Under his brief administration, Iwersen introduced the Victorian "garden cemetery" concept to Calgary. In contrast to earlier grid patterns, the garden cemetery embraced elements of nature, making use of hillside topography, curvilinear paths, and plantings that created a parklike environment. Iwersen designed the neoclassical entrance arch that still stands near its original location at the northwest corner, and erected greenhouses and a nursery to produce flowers, shrubs, and trees for use in the cemetery and in parks and boulevards across the city. He also built a new administration office and a secluded residence for the parks superintendent. But Iwersen's relationship with the City quickly soured, and he was forced to resign. He was replaced by landscape gardener William Reader, parks superintendent from 1913 to 1942 (see p. 53).

Only months after Reader's appointment the city's booming economy crashed, and within a year World War I had begun.

Reader had to make the best of lean budgets until the war was over. Over his twenty-nine year career, Reader was the singular force that transformed not only Union Cemetery, but parks, playgrounds, and boulevards across the city, into works of beauty. He created both written and photographic records of his work, which remain accessible in local archives. Reader also developed the barren area surrounding his official residence into a showcase garden with over four thousand varieties of plants, and opened it to the public in 1923. Reader Rock Garden (as it was named after his death in 1943) still adorns the northwest face of Cemetery Hill, but its manicured beauty and botanical diversity have sharply diminished. A shale clearing is all that remains of Reader's former residence.

UNION CEMETERY TODAY

With the establishment of nearby Burnsland Cemetery, Union Cemetery ceased to be Calgary's main interdenominational burying ground. As early as 1920, the parks superintendent had warned that available plots at Union were nearly exhausted. But a surprising number of markers bear late-twentieth-century dates, and funerals still take place at Union periodically. Many privately owned plots, purchased years earlier, remain unused until finally needed. In some cases private owners have sold their empty plots back to the

City, and they have become available once more for purchase. Some space also remains because of allowances for multiple burials.

Visitors to Union Cemetery need not be mourners. Consistent with the vision of Richard Iwersen and William Reader, the winding paths of Union Cemetery offer a peaceful, meditative refuge in the midst of the city's bustle. Within sight of major thoroughfares and towering skyscrapers, jackrabbits and deer browse amid cottonwood poplars, mountain ash, Scotch pines, and Colorado spruce. Mature trees shelter falcons, flickers, nesting hawks, magpies, and Hungarian partridge. Every year, decades-old peonies and lilacs still bloom over graves that might not have seen a mourner in years.

At Union Cemetery, the graves of artists and artisans, politicians and poets, and reformers and rogues, offer a tangible link to Calgary's history. However, in addition to the stories of individuals, Union Cemetery offers endless fascinating details. For example, in most early graves the head lies to the west, with the result that the body lies facing east. In western tradition, this anticipates the arrival of the Messiah in the east, and the bodily resurrection that will follow. Later graves do not necessarily follow this orientation, and some are deliberately oriented north-south to accommodate the grade of the hill or the visitor's approach from the path. Many old family plots, containing up to ten burial spaces surrounding a central monument, were once bordered by detailed iron fences that demarcated private property, even for the dead. Benevolent societies, service organizations, and unions purchased blocks of plots for use by their members, who in some cases might not otherwise have been given a proper burial. A separate area was set aside for burial of mounted police officers, and during World War I, a Field of Honour was established for military burials (see p. 49). Potter's Field, which contains a thousand graves but not a single marker, was meant for the friendless, the penniless, and the condemned (see p. 64).

Though varied in style and choice of materials, monuments are consistent with those found in similar contemporary graveyards across North America. Early monument types (see p. vi), such as columns, obelisks, pedestals, and sarcophagi, reflect a Victorian and Edwardian fascination with ancient civilizations, and hundreds of markers bear universally understood symbolic carvings (see p. 73). Granite monuments have proven the most durable, while those made of sandstone—an early local favourite, given Calgary's many sandstone quarries—have eroded badly, rendering some of the earliest epitaphs completely illegible. During and after the Great Depression, less expensive monuments of

The mortuary chapel was designed by the city engineer and completed in 1908. The contractors were Arthur Lancaster and John E. Bull. (Glenbow Archives, PD-117-13)

concrete and marble-chip conglomerate became common. Only a few crosses and two tablets remain of the forest of wooden markers that once stood in Union.

For all the monuments in Union Cemetery, there are probably just as many graves that are unmarked. In some cases the monument was damaged or removed, and in others, there never was a tombstone. Conversely, some markers simply commemorate a person buried elsewhere, or whose remains were lost. In the case of multiple burials, not everyone buried in a grave is necessarily indicated on the monument. In several instances, a monument to "my beloved wife" or "my dear husband" does not list the surviving spouse who was later interred in the same plot.

VISITING UNION CEMETERY

In the ten self-guided tours that follow, this book offers the tales of over one hundred personalities from among tens of thousands buried in Union Cemetery. The maps provided will assist in finding most graves interpreted in this book, but hillside contours, eroded epitaphs, unmarked plots, and other idiosyncrasies might lead the visitor into uncharted, though equally fascinating, territory. Concrete row markers and individual round, numbered grave markers, are helpful in locating graves, although in many cases they are hidden by grass or sod. Grave locations include three elements: lot number (plot), block number (row), and section letter (for example, 16-1-B, Colonel James F. Macleod's grave).

Visitors should take the normal precautions that would apply on any outdoor hike: sensible footwear, insect repellent, and on sunny days, a hat and water bottle. They should also be aware that by-laws require visitors to leave the cemetery by 11:00 P.M. Although a stroll through Union Cemetery can be most enjoyable, visitors should be mindful of the reverence it deserves. Graves and their monuments stand not only as a tribute to the dead, but as a relic of their times, and as such are as

precious and fragile as museum artifacts. While they may be admired and photographed, they should not be leaned or sat upon, or made subject to tombstone rubbings. Damage from erosion, force of gravity, or vandalism is not always apparent, and stones can topple or break under stress. Any vandalism should be reported to the cemetery office on site, or to the main office in Queen's Park Cemetery.

For those who wish to pursue their interest in Union Cemetery further, there are several options available. *Union Cemetery Interpretive Tour*, an illustrated booklet published by the City of Calgary Heritage Advisory Board, is distributed free at city hall, Queen's Park Cemetery, and at the Union Cemetery office in the former caretaker's cottage. Guided tours are offered by the Chinook Country Historical Society, a chapter of the Historical Society of Alberta (call 261-4667 or visit www.cadvision.com/ chinookh). Students in the Museum and Heritage Studies Program at the University of Calgary examine Union as a case study for interpretation and ethical, practical, and preservation issues. The program's practicum coordinator, Don Sucha, has developed a virtual tour of gravesites in Union and other cemeteries (www.ucalgary.ca/~dsucha/cemetery.html). Genealogical researchers can access records through the City of Calgary Archives and the Glenbow Archives. The Cemeteries Administration Office (call 221-3660) will provide grave locations, and employees at Union Cemetery can assist in locating individual graves.

Notes

1. Calgary's original Roman Catholic Cemetery moved to its present location after Union Cemetery was established. Another historic cemetery, St. Paul's Anglican in Midnapore, predates Union but remained outside the city limits until 1961.
2. *Calgary Herald*, 2 September 1883.
3. *Ibid.*, 28 September 1883.
4. *Daily Herald*, 17 June 1902.

Sections A, F, and G

1. CARNEY, ALFRED
died 1894, 23-14-A

Four years before Alfred's death, his parents Augustus and Ann Carney had farmed this very soil before it was sold and transformed into Union Cemetery. There is no available descriptive record of Alfred's funeral, but it might have been one of Augustus Carney's final visits to the old homestead. Alfred's unmarked grave is immediately south (to the left) of Jessie May Bodman's, which is marked by a small heart-shaped tablet.

2. SMITH, JAMES
circa 1864–1890, 11-12-A

For more than a century, the legend of Jimmy Smith added a tragic, but very human, story to the origin of the Calgary General Hospital. According to lore, Smith, a Chinese Canadian who had no friends or family in the city, lay dying in the Royal Hotel. Smith left his posses-sions—a sum of money variously reported as anywhere from $100 to $700 cash, and a suit of clothes—to his only visitor, the Anglican minister Reverend Cooper, asking that the money be used "to start a

The abundance of local sandstone made it a popular early choice for tombstones, but as a sedimentary stone it is easily eroded. The epitaphs are largely unreadable on this large sandstone monument, which commemorates James Barwis's wife Caroline and her mother, and the columns or urns that once adorned it have long since disappeared. (P1)

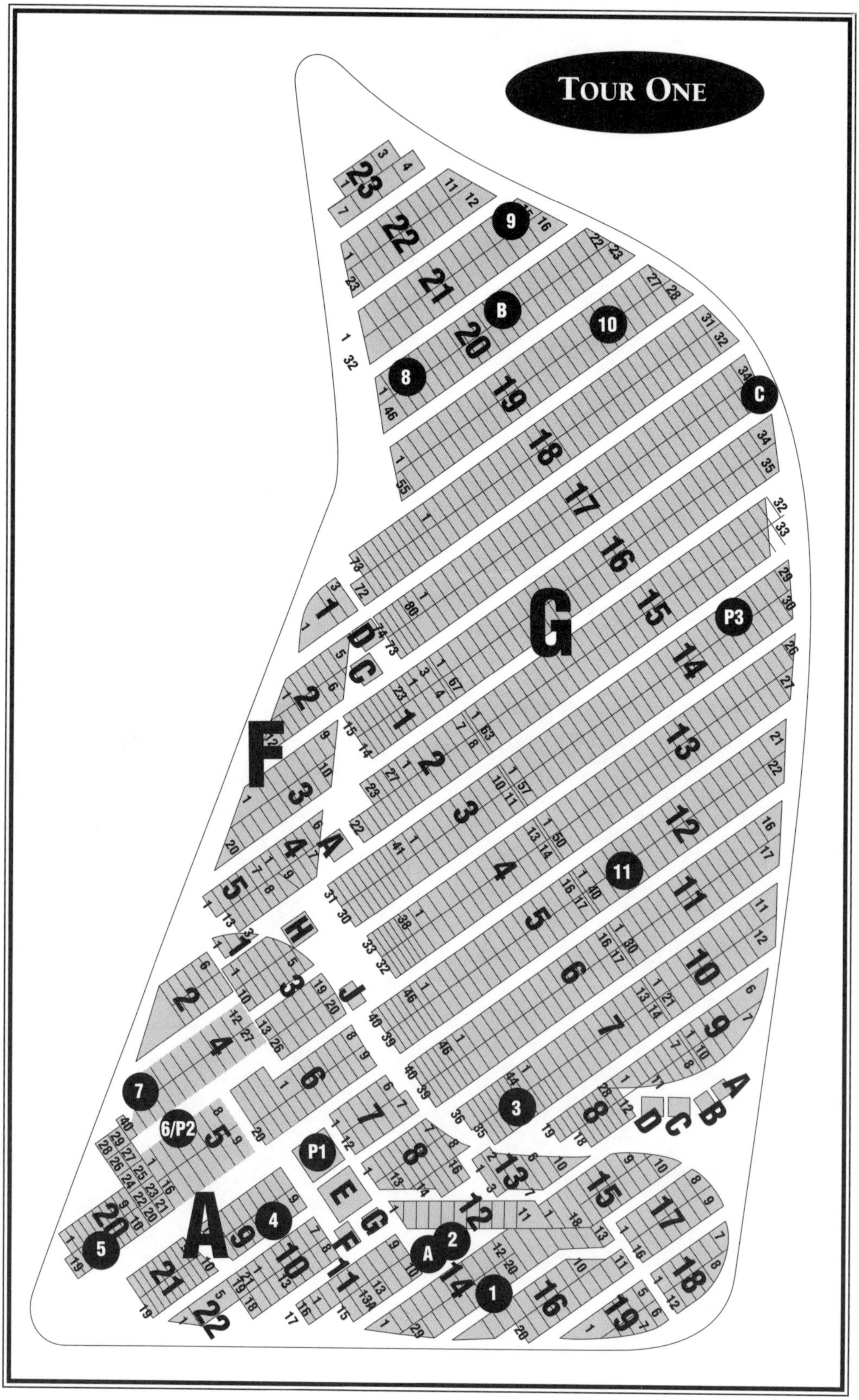
Tour One
G
F
A
P1
P3
6/P2

MAP NOTES

- ◆ Section A, one of the oldest developed areas in Union Cemetery, is a gravedigger's nightmare. With its oddly shaped plots and blocks laid out at unusual angles, it was designed with more attention to aesthetic appearance than to function. There are many unmarked graves in this section. Despite concrete block and lot markers, grave location remains more difficult in this area than anywhere else in Union Cemetery.
- ◆ Section F, the smallest in Union Cemetery, exists on its own for no apparent reason. Other sections are so designated if they are stand-alone "islands" surrounded by pathways, or if they include different types of plots than an adjacent section. Section F is functionally an extension of Section A.
- ◆ Burials in Section G began around 1904.

NOTES

A. Following his death on October 18, 1890, Quorn Ranch manager John J. Barter was one of the first people to be buried in Union Cemetery. His sandstone monument is badly eroded, but the epitaph remains legible. Barter's wife Elizabeth was the daughter of pioneer magistrate JEREMIAH TRAVIS.

B. Dr. John A. Butterwick (circa 1883–1918) was the first medical professional in Calgary to die in the worldwide Spanish influenza epidemic at the end of World War I. The epidemic claimed hundreds of lives in the city and millions worldwide.

C. A cast-metal marker, placed by the Boy Scouts of Canada and staked at the base of a lilac tree, marks the grave of Harold Van Buren Ellis (1917–30) of the 4th Calgary Troop.

hospital." Later that year, Smith's money, together with other funds, helped to rent a house on 7th Avenue and 9th Street West that became the first Calgary General Hospital. The facts of the case, uncovered by historian Frederick Hunter 110 years later, are a little happier for Mr. Smith. The former Grand Central Hotel cook did not die in a hotel, but in the care of a private nurse, and he left behind somewhere between $1,500 and $2,000, of which a large proportion was to be set aside for a General Hospital "when one is established." Smith was likely one of the last people buried at Shaganappi, and was later reinterred in Union. Smith's dilapidated tombstone was removed in 1922; his unmarked grave can be found two lots northeast (to the right) of Barkly Higginson.

3. BATES, WILLIAM STANLEY
1872–1949, 32-7-G

One of Calgary's best-known early architects, William Stanley Bates was born in Yorkshire and moved to Calgary in 1904. His firm's commissions included a large number of banks, churches, commercial buildings, hospitals, hotels, residences, and schools in Calgary and across southern Alberta. Bates designed the Grain Exchange Building, Calgary's first skyscraper, for developer William Roper Hull. Built in 1909 and still standing at 815 - 1st Street SW, the Grain Exchange is considered Calgary's first "truly modern business block." A grey granite tablet marks the grave Bates shares with his wife Marion. Though better known as an artist, their son Maxwell also studied architecture; perhaps his best-known commission is St. Mary's Cathedral, completed in 1956.

4. HALLIDAY, TENA STEVENSON
circa 1869–1892, 7-9-A

In the summer of 1892, Calgary suffered a smallpox outbreak. The first occurrence was detected in late June in a Chinese laundry, and many citizens unfairly blamed the epidemic on Calgary's tiny Chinese community. Tensions mounted after twenty-three-year-old Tena Halliday died of smallpox on July 22, only a few days after giving birth to a son. Her husband, baker William James Halliday, was among the many Calgarians who were quarantined. Violence finally erupted on August 2, when a mob of three hundred drunken men attacked Chinese Calgarians and their property. The NWMP quickly dispersed the crowd, but ill feelings remained. William Halliday survived the epidemic and later remarried. Tena is buried with their baby Freddie, who died on August 8. A towering red granite obelisk marks their grave.

5. DOUGHTY, EDWARD
circa 1858–1940, 16-20-A

During the Great Depression, the education of schoolchildren was not complete without a visit to the Calgary Public Museum, housed in the North-West Travellers Building (515 - 1st Street SE) from 1928 to 1935. Shropshire-born Edward Doughty, a former grocer and businessman, served as its enthusiastic curator for most of the museum's existence. The crowded galleries featured art displays, historical artifacts (among them Oliver Cromwell's glasses, said to be "fine for almost everything except seeing through"),[1] and natural history exhibits (including a cross-sectioned, working beehive). Hailed as one of only five such municipally operated institutions in Canada, the Calgary Public Museum provided a free educational opportunity during the worst years of the Depression. Despite its constant shortage of funds, the museum never charged admission.

Doughty put all his old salesman's skills to use drumming up donations, even though he was paid poorly and irregularly for his labours. By 1935 government funding and large-scale donations had evaporated, and Doughty closed the doors for the final time. A small white stone with a lamb in relief memorializes his two children who predeceased him, but not Doughty himself.

6. PEARCE, WILLIAM
1848–1930, 4-5-A

Surveyor, civil engineer, and senior civil servant, William Pearce has been described as "a man who did more to develop the vast inland empire of western Canada than any man of his time."[2] Canadian nationalists remember Pearce as one of the surveyors who in 1874 established the 49th parallel, which forms much of the Canada-U.S. boundary. Others recall his key role in the creation of the national parks system in 1885. Calgarians can thank him for the creation of Mewata and

A boulder, part of a glacial erratic, marks the grave of surveyor, civil engineer, and senior civil servant William Pearce. His signature is engraved in the stone. (P2)

Memorial parks, and for civic ownership of the islands in the Bow River, including the present site of the Calgary Zoo. As Inspector of Dominion Land Agencies and Superintendent of Mines, Pearce had vast responsibilities for land use and resource development throughout the Northwest Territories. He moved to Calgary around 1887, and remained for the rest of his life. After leaving the federal civil service in 1904, Pearce worked for the CPR until he retired in 1926.

7. WINN, JAMES
1837–1911, 1-4-A

During the first decade of the twentieth century, agricultural settlers filled the prairies, and many of the newcomers passed through the offices of James Winn, Dominion government immigration officer for Calgary. Born in Coburg, Ontario, Winn moved to Calgary in 1891 and received his government appointment in 1899, holding it until his death a dozen years later. Winn earned a reputation for both efficiency and compassion. According to the *Albertan*, his thorough knowledge of conditions in the province "was always at the disposal of the newly arrived immigrants, and many a family of new-comers owe their prosperity in their new homes to the kindly words of advice and encouragement given them by Immigration Officer James Winn."[3] En route to his funeral, a chain of mourners—particularly Winn's Masonic brethren—stretched half a mile long. The pediment of Winn's balmoral red granite screen emphasized the Masonic symbol. To the right, a grey marble tablet with the image of an open gateway, symbolizing heaven, marks the grave of Winn's first wife, Jane Mills (circa 1850–97).

8. BLOW, THOMAS HENRY
1862–1932, 2-20-G

Calgary's pioneer eye, ear, nose, and throat specialist was born in South Mountain, Ontario, and earned a medical degree at McGill. He arrived in Calgary in 1903, two years before the province of Alberta was formed. When Edmonton became the capital, many expected that Calgary would get the provincial university. An educated professional, Blow was bitterly disappointed when the University of Alberta went to Strathcona—a city later absorbed by Edmonton. Blow and a prominent group of businessmen, including William Tregillus (buried nearby in 1-21-A), tried to found a private university. He personally donated forty thousand dollars for the endowment and served as the Chairman of the Board of Calgary College from 1912 to 1915, the entire life of the institution. Calgary College held classes in the public library, but under its provincial charter it lacked the power to grant degrees. Blow fought for the college as an opposition Conservative MLA (1913–23), but the school folded after only three years. Impressed by Calgary's efforts, the provincial government established the Provincial Institute of Technology and Art (later renamed the Southern Alberta Institute of Technology, or SAIT) in 1916. Blow died during the Great Depression; after World War II his Mount Royal residence became a convalescent home for returned soldiers. Blow shares his monument, a Dakota mahogany granite screen topped by a double pediment, with others in the family plot. An image of a camping trailer adorns Lillian Blow's footstone.

9. MOREY, LUCILLE FRANCIS
1909–1911, 15-21-G

A simple grey granite tablet marks the grave of Lucille Morey, who lived with her parents near Fire Hall No. 1, on the present site of Royal Canadian Legion No. 1. There, Fire Chief James "Cappy" Smart kept a menagerie of animals that included a grizzly bear, Noodles, and a "cinnamon" bear, Major. Cappy enjoyed boxing with Major, but warned of the animal's increasingly savage disposition after it killed and ate two puppies. Smart expressed fear for the children who played around the fire hall. One of them was little Lucille, who only a day after being warned to stay away from Major, ventured too close and was mauled to death. Both Noodles and Major were put down.

Tiny shoes and a single stocking stand in relief on the white marble tombstone of Hattie C. Gibbs, the five-year-old daughter of William James Gibbs, who died in 1909. (P3)

10. SOMERVILLE, WILLIAM
1849–1925, 22-19-G

Ontario-born William Somerville first visited Calgary in the 1890s as a traveller for his brother Tom's Somerville Monument Company, based in Brandon, Manitoba. William settled permanently in Calgary in 1903 and, with assistance from his brother Herbert, set up his own monument firm. By 1911, William's Calgary-based Somerville Company and its Calgary Granite & Marble Works had at least twenty-five employees and a trade area that extended throughout Alberta, British Columbia, and Saskatchewan. A large number of monuments in Union Cemetery were manufactured by Somerville or by its early rival, the Albert J. Hart Monument Co. Somerville's company outlived his death and remains a significant local concern. William's unobtrusive pillow marker, made from balmoral red granite, contrasts sharply with the imposing monuments he created for so many others.

11. GOWEN, GEORGE HARRISON
circa 1840–1910, 36-12-G

The only known veteran of the American Civil War (1861–65) buried in Union Cemetery fought on the Confederate side. Born at St. Simon's Island, Georgia, Gowen served as a 1st Sergeant in Company D of the 4th Georgia Cavalry. Little is known about him from the time his service ended until his death at Shepard, Alberta, near Calgary. His grey marble tablet reads "Confederate Veteran of the Am. Civil War." Gowen's wife Edith is buried with him.

Notes

1. *Calgary Daily Herald*, 15 December 1934.
2. *Albertan*, 16 September 1975.
3. *Morning Albertan*, 23 January 1911.

Section M

1. COCHRANE, FITZGERALD
1831–1886, 25-18-M

Halifax-born Fitz Cochrane, one of the first lawyers to settle in Calgary, cemented his reputation in the young town's second murder trial, held in June 1884. James McManus stood accused of killing Billy Reed, alias "Buckskin Shorty," in a drunken brawl outside the town limits. After Cochrane's eloquent defence, the jury acquitted McManus of murder, but convicted him of manslaughter. Cochrane's promising career ended with his premature death from a stroke less than two years later. He was the first person in what is now Alberta to be buried with full Masonic rites; each fellow Mason at the funeral placed a sprig of evergreen in his grave. Cochrane's body was reinterred at Union in 1911, probably one of the last moved from Shaganappi Cemetery. In 1991, Masons from Loyalty Lodge No. 197 placed a serpentine tablet monument on his previously unmarked grave.

2. INTHOUT, GRACE M.
circa 1890–1912, 88-11-M

At the height of the city's phenomenal boom, and only weeks after the original, legendary 1912 Stampede, Calgarians were shocked by a suicide pact carried out in the Queen's Hotel, on the present site of the Calgary Municipal Building. William Inthout was a thirty-year-old telegraph operator from Paintsville, Kentucky. He worked in the Yukon before moving to Garfield, Washington, where he met twenty-two-year-old Grace Brunell. The two married in Spokane in August 1912, then moved to Fernie, British Columbia, where William found work. He evidently took to drink, lost his job, argued publicly with Grace and struck her. Impulsively, the Inthouts boarded a train for Calgary, checked into the Queen's, and bought a .32 calibre revolver. That evening the bellboy brought six glasses of whisky to their room. At 11:30 p.m. the sound of three gunshots threw the hotel guests into "a paroxysm of terror."[1] The night clerk, accompanied by police, found the Inthouts lying embraced in their bed, dead or dying from gunshot wounds. Correspondence found in the room shed some light on the tragedy, but also created new mysteries. In an unmailed letter, Grace wrote to her mother: "We loved each other to the end. Billy killed Dutro because he lied about me. We have decided to end it."[2] A letter addressed to William and mailed from Oregon suggests a further crime: "Lawler has written the company of the condition of his daughter, and says she is only fifteen years old, and one of the company's detectives is here....They are under the impression that you are in California or South America....Depend upon me not giving you away."[3] Details of the Oregon girl and the enigmatic Dutro remain a mystery. The couple's last wish, to be buried together, was denied. Grace's unmarked grave is two lots south of William Jones. William Inthout's body was evidently shipped to Paintsville.

Tour Two

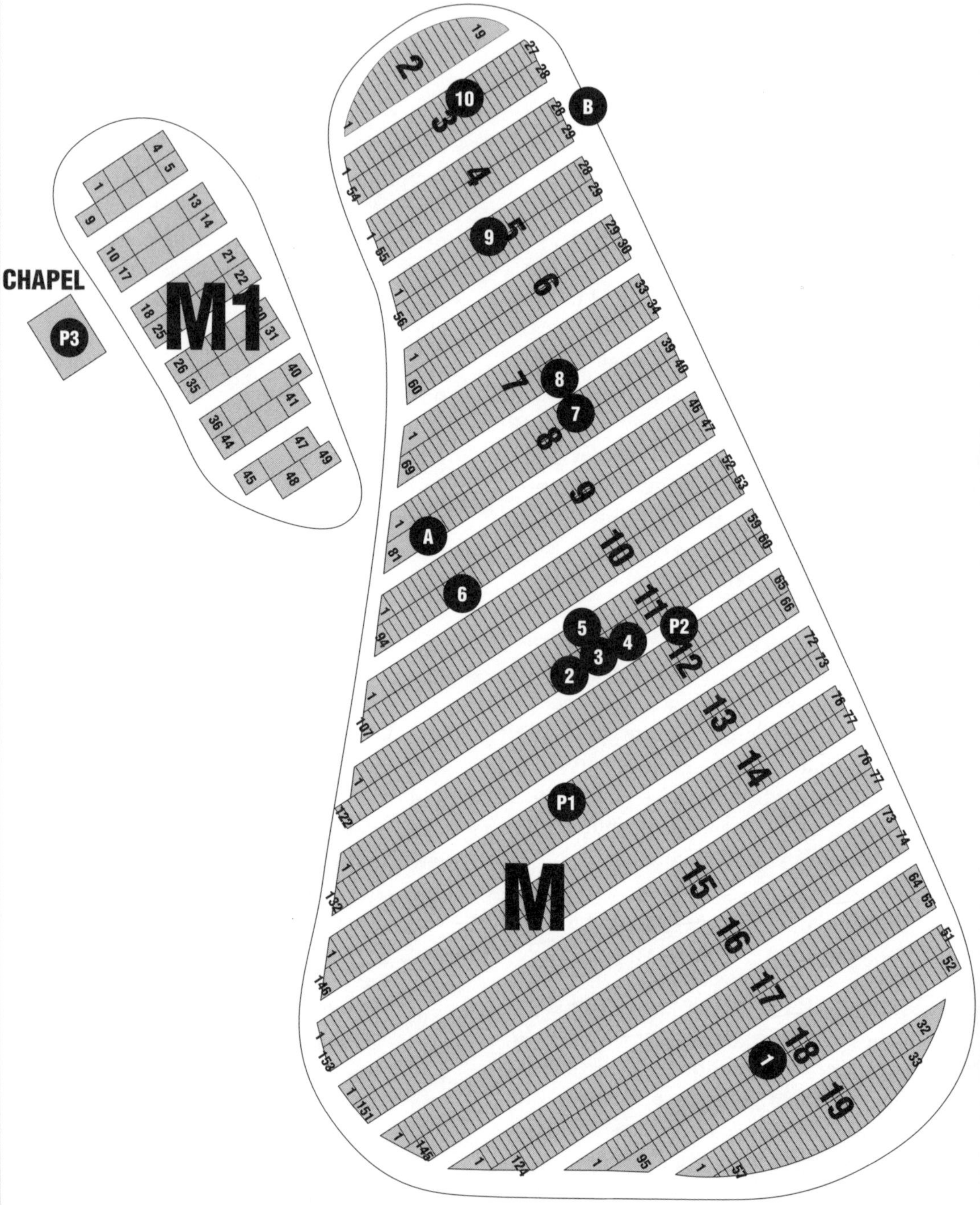
CHAPEL
P3
M1
M
A
B
P1
P2

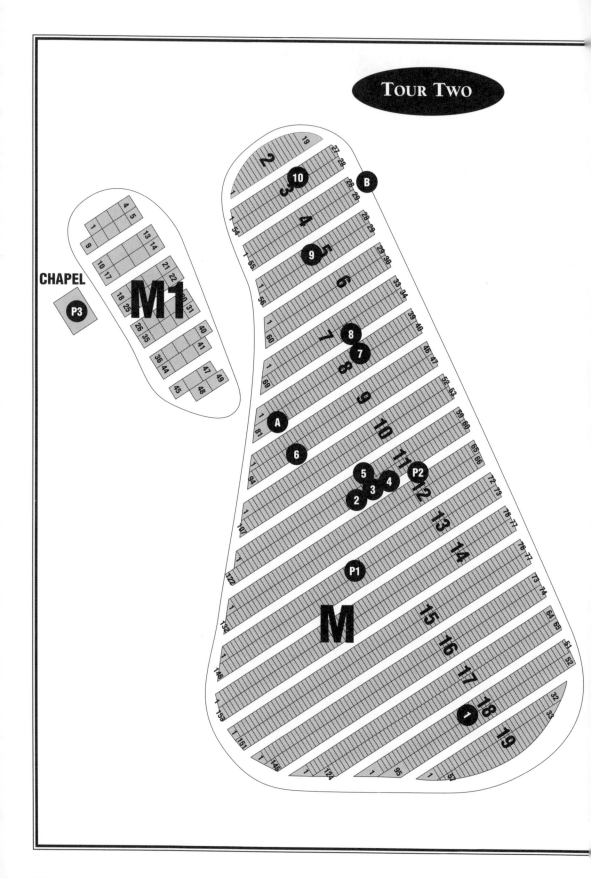

3. DAVIS, JOHN C.
died 1912, 85-11-M;

4. DAVIS, MINNIE
circa 1888–1912, 84-11-M;

5. DIXON, MILDRED
circa 1887–1912, 33-11-M

Only weeks after the tragic suicides of William and Grace M. Inthout, Calgarians were shocked by a double murder-suicide that dominated local headlines for days. The central figure was John C. Davis, an Alabaman who had moved to Calgary around 1906 and established a successful real estate business. The second figure was Minnie Black, a young waitress originally from Belfast. Minnie had been involved in a much-publicized police scandal in 1910, when she accused a police

officer of sexual advances but declined to appear as a witness against him. The third was Mildred Dixon, a twenty-five-year-old stenographer from Edinburgh who worked as a private detective at the Capital Detective Agency. Davis met Black at the restaurant where she worked, and the two eloped in 1911. Before long, John became obsessively jealous and was convinced Minnie was cheating on him. Minnie left John after he became abusive and started locking her in the house, but he persuaded her to return. John then hired Mildred Dixon to shadow Minnie. The detective moved into the boarding house where the Davises lived, but quickly realized that John was abusive and that his suspicions were groundless. Disobeying her employers, Mildred told Minnie the whole story and persuaded her to leave John. For protection, Minnie moved into Mildred's apartment in a building that still stands at 602 - 17th Avenue SW. The jealous husband found the two women and tried to speak to his wife. He even rented a room in the neighbouring building so he could spy on Minnie through the window. Fearing for their safety, the women went to the police, but Minnie refused to press charges. Finally, John promised to leave Minnie alone forever and return to the United States, but he wanted to meet with her one more time. He arrived at Mildred's apartment with a .38 calibre revolver. It is uncertain whether John was admitted to the room or forced his way in, but he was heard to shout, "For God's sake Minnie, don't leave me!"[4] He shot and killed his wife, mortally wounded the detective, then committed suicide. Mildred died the following day. In a bizarre postscript, it was revealed a month later that John Davis was actually Spencer Holder, a bigamist who had abandoned his wife and two children in Alabama. The Davises are buried side by side in unmarked graves; John is buried immediately north of William Jones, and the next grave to the north is Minnie's. Mildred's unmarked grave is in the next row to the west, immediately north of Frank C. Tuffin.

6. FISK, JOHN C.
1874–1911, 84-9-M

Born near Walkerton, Ontario, Jack Fisk moved west at the turn of the century, and in 1902 purchased a ranch near Gladys, Alberta. The young bachelor was well liked by his neighbours, whom he got to know as the local agent for an American supply firm. One of those neighbours was Tucker Peach, a misanthropic old rancher who distrusted banks and reportedly hoarded all his money in his cabin. When Peach disappeared in May 1910, he was believed to have sold his land to Thomas Robertson, a CPR brakeman, and moved back to England. That summer a decomposed, headless corpse was found along the Bow River near Brooks, and in November 1910

Frank and M.E. Webster lost two young children within a few months in 1910. This beautifully sculpted stone memorializes Frankie and Marjory Webster. (P1)

a human skull with a bullet hole through it was found nearby. The skull had the mark of an old forehead injury, corresponding to the spot where Peach had been kicked by a horse a quarter century earlier. Confronted by police, Robertson eventually confessed to the crime, but alleged that Fisk had proposed that the two men murder Peach; Robertson was to have the land and Fisk would take the horses and money. According to Robertson, the two men entered Peach's cabin on May 9, 1910. Fisk shot first, then Robertson, and they dumped the body in the river. Robertson was sentenced to life in prison and Fisk was hanged on June 27, 1911, though doubt still exists as to his guilt. Besides his alleged victim (in plot 20-20-G, an unmarked grave two lots south of Pearl A Brownell, wife of R.T. McLoskey), Fisk's prosecutor (James Short, 2-1-L [West]) and the judge who condemned him (Charles A. Stuart, 11-2-K) are also buried in Union Cemetery. Fisk's grave is unmarked, but is located directly east of William Gillett. After Fisk's execution, the Mounted Police took possession of his dog and named him "Fisk". The dog befriended Constable Francis Walter "Happy" Davies (buried in 32-8-D), and was present when his new master was murdered in 1912. The dog's third master, Corporal A. F. C. Watts, survived a gunfight at Exshaw—with "Fisk" at his side. "Fisk" was hit by a car and killed in 1919.

7. BARR, ROBERT
died 1913, 25-8-M

Between 1911 and 1914, hundreds of men worked on the construction of the CPR's Palliser Hotel, Calgary's largest and most luxurious hostelry. One July afternoon in 1913, plumber's helper Robert Barr was on the fourth floor waiting for a lift that was bringing sinks from the basement. He peered down the shaft to look for the elevator—which was descending from above.

It knocked Barr on the head and sent him tumbling to the bottom of the shaft. He died in hospital of a fractured skull. Barr's spirit plays a small role in Aritha van Herk's 1998 novel *Restlessness*, which is set in the hotel. His unmarked grave is located to the right of Alfred Wright.

8. HOWARTH, BEATRICE
died 1914, 48-7-M

On May 28, 1914, the CPR steamship *Empress of Ireland* set sail from Quebec City to Liverpool. Only hours into the voyage, the *Empress* entered a fog and collided with a Norwegian coal ship, the Storstad. The *Empress* sank into the cold waters of the St. Lawrence in only fourteen minutes, taking over a thousand people—including third-class passengers Beatrice Howarth and her children Emmie and Leonard—to a watery death. The loss of the *Empress* was Canada's worst maritime disaster in peace-time. Beatrice's husband, bricklayer R.H. Howarth, had travelled with his family as far as Quebec City, and saw them for the last time when the *Empress* left the harbour. A small marble tablet reads "DROWNED ON THE / EMPRESS OF IRELAND."

9. CARTER, CHARLES
circa 1894–1914, 14-5-M

At 7:00 p.m. on March 16, 1914, employees at the Mitchell Bakery on 17th Avenue were at their busiest when the light in front of the oven began to flicker. Baker James Thom tried to turn it off, while his colleague Charles Carter went behind the oven to throw the main switch. Suddenly the bakery was plunged into darkness and both men fell to the floor. "I'm killed, I'm killed,"[5] Carter said. The other employees brought lights into the shop and found Carter lying dead and Thom suffering from electrical shock. Carter had evidently created a deadly circuit by touching the metal oven at the same time as the switch. The

Both this tablet and the dove atop it are carved from a single block of grey marble. It marks the grave of Stewart G. Goodfellow, the young son of Walter and Isabella. (P2)

problem was caused by a high voltage wire at 17th Avenue and 5th Street SE—a residential area now within Stampede Park—that accidentally made contact with a lighting service wire. The Mitchell Bakery was by no means the only place affected. Small fires erupted throughout the high voltage district along 17th Avenue SE, and streetlights in the area went down. Fourteen-year-old Roy Taylor burned his hand and foot trying to turn on a kitchen light, and stable foreman William Woods died of electrocution while switching out the light in a horse barn. Carter and Woods were the only fatalities in the incident. Carter had moved to Calgary from Canterbury, England in about 1912. His unmarked grave is immediately south of Laila B. Sheffield.

An excellent example of a lamb sculpture, commonly seen on children's graves, near the mortuary chapel in Section M1. (P3)

10. GARNETT, WILLIAM AND MARY
died 1914, 17-3-M

Like Beatrice Howarth and her children, William and Mary Garnett were third class passengers aboard the doomed *Empress of Ireland.* The Garnetts were among scores of members of the Salvation Army aboard the ship, on their way to London for an international conference. The Garnetts left five children behind, including son Willie, who reportedly awoke the morning after the disaster—before he had heard the news—and shouted "Oh, my poor mother!"[6] William Garnett had brought with him his life insurance documents—including receipts—to sort out a difficulty with the insurance company in England. How the matter was resolved remains unknown. The Garnetts' white marble-shouldered tablet reads "LOST ON THE / EMPRESS OF IRELAND." Their son William (1901–64) is buried next to them.

Notes
1. *Calgary News-Telegram,* 21 September 1912.
2. *Calgary Daily Herald,* 21 September 1912.
3. *Ibid.*
4. *Morning Albertan,* 7 October 1912.
5. *Calgary News-Telegram,* 17 March 1914.
6. *Morning Albertan,* 30 May 1914.

Sections E, H, J, and K

1. WOOD, ALICE DEVOLIN
circa 1875–1908, 17-2-K

Between 1904 and 1908, Alice Devolin Wood's Calgary Rescue Home provided badly-needed assistance and shelter to hundreds of single mothers and their children, reaching out to "fallen women" (prostitutes) and "betrayed girls" (unwed mothers). Born in Madoc, Ontario, Alice K. Devolin married George E. Wood around 1901. Though Alice loved children, she had none of her own. The *Daily News* eulogized her as "Calgary's greatest benefactor," noting that "today while she sleeps in death five babes and two little girls are crying for their foster mother, whose

tenderness knew no bounds but which responds no more to human need."[2] She was thirty-three years old. "*HER MEMORY IS BLESSED*" reads the epitaph on her Vermont grey marble marker, which also notes her accomplishment.

2. McNEILL, LEISHMAN
1896–1964, (58-59)-1-K

For a generation of Calgarians, broadcaster and columnist Jack Peach (1913–93) was an unparalleled font of popular local history, sharing his memories, insights, and gentle humour through several books and countless newspaper columns. Leishman McNeill was the Jack Peach of his day. The

The McArthur family's impressive monument, with relief lettering and floral imagery is unique in Union Cemetery and might have been inspired by ancient sarcophagi. (P1)

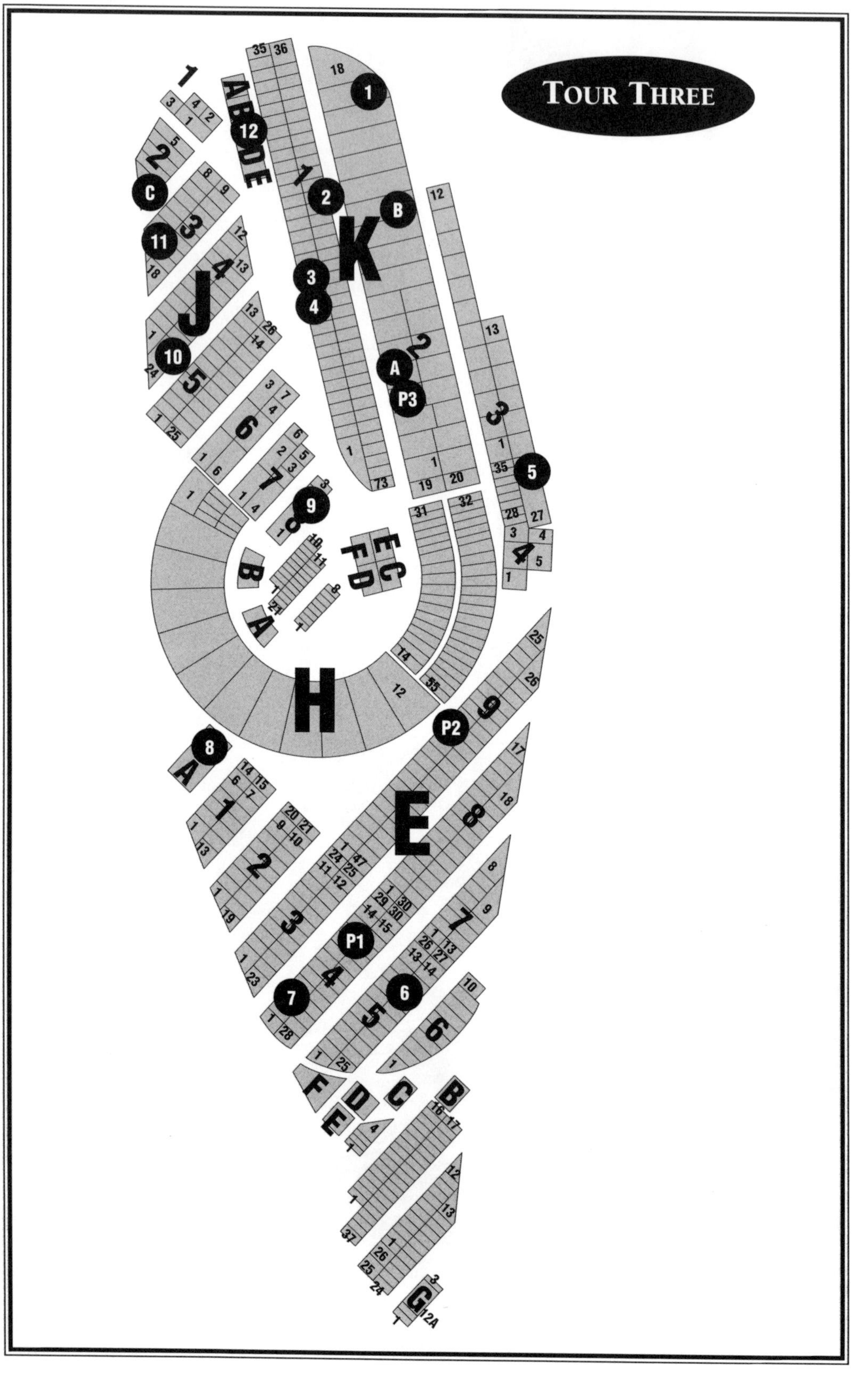
TOUR THREE
K
J
H
E
G
P1
P2
P3

Map Notes

- Topography distinguishes the four sections that share this "island" in the cemetery. Section H wraps in a semicircle around the brow of this hill, Sections J and K cling to its slopes, and Section E occupies the bottom of the hill.
- Section H comprises a single block, and contains the largest plots in the entire cemetery. Some of its plots can contain as many as twelve graves.
- In flat areas of city cemeteries, blocks are laid out with head-to-head graves, which allows for a single row of back-to-back monuments. In hilly areas such as this, graves are set out head-to-foot, necessitating two rows of monuments in each block. Most hillside graves in Union Cemetery are oriented to the east, facing the sunrise.

Notes

A. From 1911 to 1921, J. F. M. (Frank) Moodie (1878–1943) managed the Rosedale Coal & Clay Products near Drumheller. He assembled what the *Calgary Herald* called "one of the finest collections of minerals and precious stones on the continent."[1] Appropriately, Moodie's grave is decorated by a petrified stump.

B. In 1917, as a justice of Supreme Court of Alberta, Charles Allan Stuart (1864–1926) upheld the appointment of women as magistrates—a judgment affecting the appointment of ALICE JAMIESON and Emily Murphy. In 1908 he became the first chancellor of the University of Alberta, a position he held until his death. Justice Stuart sentenced JOHN C. FISK to death in 1911.

C. One of the most touching epitaphs in Union Cemetery appears on a tiny marker in the Birney family plot. Private Frederick William Copas (1896–1917) lies buried in a Canadian war cemetery in Pas-de-Calais, France. His memorial in Union reads simply: "IN MEMORY OF / DEAR OLD FRED / KILLED IN ACTION / VIMY RIDGE / APRIL 9, 1917 / AGED 21 YEARS".

son of a pioneer Calgary building contractor, McNeill grew up with the city, and his contemporaries were the sons and daughters of its pioneers. In 1950, McNeill wrote a series of *Calgary Herald* columns titled "Tales of the Old Town," reprinted in anthology form after his death. Though not a professional historian, McNeill's personal observations record details of early Calgary and its citizens that otherwise would have been lost. A concrete retaining wall marks the perimeter of the McNeill family plot.

3. LOUISE RILEY
1900–1957, (16-17)-1-K

Anyone who grew up in Calgary in the 1930s and 1940s knew the tall, storytelling librarian in the Calgary Public Library's children's department. Besides developing the library's collection of children's books, she contributed to the genre with *The Mystery Horse* and *Train for Tiger Lily*. She also wrote a novel for adults, *One Happy Moment*. Louise read children's stories on a weekly radio program and initiated an adolescent section in the library. She was promoted to assistant chief librarian in 1949. The Calgary Public Library named a new branch library for Louise Riley after her death. Her grey granite marker is a western slant memorial with rustic rockshell. Louise is buried in the Riley family plot, not far from her father, Ezra Riley, who donated Riley Park to the City in 1910.

A sandstone retaining wall surrounds the hillside grave of John Donohue (circa 1854–1907), Mountie turned hotel-keeper and founder of an early private "zoo." Images of a bird and a stag's head stand in relief on his pedestal marker. (P2)

4. HALL, MARY ELIZA
circa 1871–1907, 14-1-K

Before the Mount Royal district was annexed to Calgary in 1907, a small group of wealthy American families built their homes on this scenic suburban hillside, which some people were already calling American Hill. Among the residents were Mary Hall and her husband Edward George, owner of the Alberta Nursery & Seed Company. Since their home lay outside the city limits, the Halls dug their own well and installed a gasoline-powered pump. One summer evening in 1907, while E. G. had gone to town, Mary noticed a gas leak in the basement and went down to fix it. "What happened then no person knows," the *Morning Albertan* reported the next day.[3] The house filled with black smoke; seven-year-old Sarah Hall rescued her baby sister, and neighbours braved the smoke to retrieve Mary, who was fatally burned from a gas explosion. She remained conscious, but died later in hospital. The Hall house stood at 2106 Hope Street SW until it was demolished in 1993. Mary's grave is unmarked; it lies just outside the Riley family plot, next to Louise Riley.

5. HONENS, ESTHER
1903–1992, 21-3-K

The founder of the Esther Honens Calgary International Piano Competition Foundation was born Esther Smith in Pittsburgh, Pennsylvania, and moved to Calgary with her parents in 1908. She spent a quarter century working for Birks Jewellers, much of it as office manager. Esther married realtor Jack Hiller (1884–1967) in 1950, and later as a widow married rancher Harry Honens (1895–1994). She made a considerable fortune in real estate, and late in life donated five million dollars to establish a world-class competition "to identify the finest of today's young pianists, to bring them to Calgary for a competition that will be held in the highest international esteem and to create a legacy of musical excellence that can be enjoyed by Canadians for countless generations"[4] She lived just long enough to see her dream come true. A mountain rose granite tablet marks her grave.

6. YEOMANS, AMELIA
1842–1913, 17-5-E

After the death of her husband Augustus, a U.S. army surgeon and Civil War veteran, thirty-eight-year-old Amelia Yeomans enrolled in medicine at the University of Michigan, where her daughter Lillian was already a medical student. Lillian became Winnipeg's first female physician, and Amelia the second. She practised for six-teen years, specializing in women's and children's diseases. A social reformer and temperance advocate, she founded the Manitoba Suffrage Club and became vice-president of the Dominion Women's Christian Temperance Union. Amelia had retired from medicine by the time she moved to Calgary in 1905, but remained active in the temperance and women's suffrage movements. She was honorary president of the Calgary Women's Suffrage Association. Amelia is buried with her daughter, Florence Cairns, who prede-ceased her. A floral pattern is etched on each side of her granite pedestal.

7. CROSS, ALFRED ERNEST
1861–1932, 3-4-E

Montreal-born A.E. Cross trained as a vet-erinarian before moving west in 1884 and entering the ranching business. In 1892 Cross and a small group of businessmen established the Calgary Brewing and Malting Company, a major employer and significant producer of beer and other beverages. In 1912, American promoter Guy Weadick asked Cross and three other wealthy ranchers to provide financial back-ing for a "Frontier Week" celebration. Weadick's idea became the Calgary Stampede, and Cross and his colleagues have been immortalized as the Big Four. Cross is the only member of the group buried in Union Cemetery. His monolithic tablet is made of Swedish black granite; the horizontal grave cover is grey granite. Cross' wife Helen (1878–1959), daughter of Colonel JAMES FARQUHARSON MACLEOD, is buried beside him. Her epitaph suggests she was the "first white child," presumably in southern Alberta.

8. OSBORNE, FREDERICK ERNEST
1878–1948, A1-E

For Fred Osborne, a youthful job as a bookstore errand boy was the start of a life-long career in the book business. In 1905 he left his native Belleville, Ontario for Calgary and founded a landmark business on 8th Avenue. Osborne's Books also carried stationery supplies, music, British newspapers, and magazines, and had a lending library service before the Calgary Public Library existed. "If you cannot see the samples at our store," Osborne's adver-tised, "we will be glad to show them to you at your residence."[5] Generations of Calgarians bought schoolbooks at Osborne's, the most important textbook dealer in southern Alberta. Osborne was elected to city council in 1918 and served as mayor from 1927 to 1929. Osborne was awarded the Order of the British Empire for his work with the National War Finance Committee during World War II. Osborne's Books outlived him, but was destroyed by fire in 1966. The Osborne family marker is a grey granite monolithic tablet; Osborne's footstone is white marble.

9. HULL, WILLIAM ROPER
1856–1925, 2-8-J

In 1873, young William Roper Hull and his brother John quit England for the life of stock raising in Canada's west. After a large cattle drive to Calgary in 1884, Hull decided to settle in the growing town. The brothers built up a business that included ranches, a slaughterhouse, and a chain of retail meat stores before going their separate ways in 1896. Hull sold his meat business to Patrick Burns in 1905, but remained one of Calgary's most significant businessmen and developers. He built the magnificent Hull's Opera House in 1893 and the city's first skyscraper, the Grain Exchange Building, in 1909. Hull was also one of the businessmen behind ALFRED ERNEST CROSS' Calgary Brewing and Malting Company in 1892. His widow Emmeline lived in their stately 13th Avenue mansion, Langmore, until her death in 1953. The Hulls had no children, but willed a large portion of their estate to establish and maintain the William Roper Hull Home for orphaned and troubled children. Among

A single sandstone block is all that remains of the Sproat family mausoleum, dismantled in the 1980s. (P3)

the symbols carved into the Hulls' grey granite memorial are Union Jacks, a torch symbolizing life, and a wreath.

10. EDWORTHY, THOMAS
1856–1904, 23-4-J

One of Calgary's first market gardeners. Thomas Edworthy left England in his teens, settling first in Ontario, then taking up ranching west of Calgary in 1883. Edworthy's original 1883 house, which he built of Douglas fir logs, still stands in the park that bears his name. His land also included part of the present Wildwood district. Sandstone deposits on his land allowed Edworthy to establish the Bow Bank Sandstone Quarries, which helped transform pre-World War I Calgary into a sandstone city. In 1897 he married Mary Ross, widow of photographer ALEXANDER J. ROSS. Thomas died of typhoid in 1904. A granite family headstone stands behind his sloping pillow marker, which identifies Thomas and Mary as "CALGARY PIONEERS / 1883 AND 1886".

11. WARE, JOHN
1850–1905, (1-4)-3-J

Born a slave in South Carolina, John Ware won his freedom in 1865 with the Union victory in the American Civil War. He moved to Texas and became a highly skilled cowboy. Ware participated in large cattle drives to Montana and Alberta, where he eventually settled and worked on the well-known Bar U and Quorn ranches. He later became a rancher in his own right, first near Sheep Creek, and later near Brooks, and built up a herd of almost a thousand head of cattle. He bought this family plot in the spring of 1905, after the death of his wife Mildred (1871–1905). Only months later, Ware was killed when his horse stumbled and fell on him. A blue pearl granite pedestal, topped by a pediment, marks the Ware family plot.

12. RILEY, ALPHA MAUDE
1880–1962, C-K;

RILEY, HAROLD WILLIAM
1877–1946, C-K

An extraordinary number of babies and young children are buried at Union Cemetery, a testament to early Calgary's high rate of infant mortality. Child labour, disease, poor sanitation, deficient health care, and an absence of playgrounds brought misery and even death to thousands of young souls. Their champion, the *Calgary Herald* later wrote, came as "a plump little tyrant with winning ways who charms (or bullies) governments—local, provincial and federal—into passing legislation for the welfare of children."[6] Maude Keen left her native Ontario to teach in Nose Creek, Alberta, but resigned in 1907 to marry Harold W. Riley. Two years later, at the point of death after giving birth to her first child, Maude made a pact with God. If she survived, Maude would dedicate her life to children's welfare. As President of the Alberta Council on Child and Family Welfare for thirty-nine years, her focus ranged from health education and free hospital care to subsidized housing, criminal justice reform, and rating of motion pictures. Maude's associates and friends were a who's who of Canadian social reformers, including Marion Carson,

Henrietta Muir Edwards, Louise McKinney, and Irene Parlby. When Harold died in 1946, Maude moved into the Palliser Hotel. Their house was converted into the Maude Riley Home, a children's shelter. Her epitaph reads: "DEVOTED TO CHILD WELFARE".

Born in St. Lambert, Quebec, young Harold W. Riley moved to Calgary with his parents and his brother, Ezra H. Riley, and grew up on the family farm in what is now the Hillhurst district. Harold was the first registrar of the University of Alberta, held elected office as an alderman and MLA, and was at one time the youngest deputy minister in Canada. He became secretary-treasurer of the Calgary Stock Exchange, and was one of the founders of the Southern Alberta Pioneers and Their Descendants. His epitaph reads "ALBERTA PIONEER AND OLDTIMER". Harold and Maude Riley share a green granite horizontal tablet with rounded checks.

Notes
1. *Calgary Herald*, 25 June 1943.
2. *Calgary Daily News*, 5 February 1908.
3. *Morning Albertan*, 15 July 1907.
4. *Calgary Herald*, 4 December 1992.
5. *Calgary Daily Herald*, 12 November 1910.
6. *Calgary Herald*, 24 April 1954.

TOUR FOUR

Section B

1. LIVINGSTON, SAMUEL HENRY HARKWOOD
1831–1897, 16-9-B

Though he shares the title "Calgary's first citizen" with GEORGE CLIFT KING, Sam Livingston and his kin were uniquely "Calgary's first family." While still in his teens, Livingston (frequently misspelled "Livingstone", including on his tombstone) left his native Ireland and joined both the California gold rush of 1849 and British Columbia's Cariboo gold rush in 1858. Livingston married Jane Howse in 1864, and nine years later they opened a trading post on the future Calgary townsite. In 1875, only months before the NWMP arrived to establish Fort Calgary, the Livingstons homesteaded upstream on the Elbow River. Sam was the first settler to bring mechanical farming equipment to the Calgary area. With his buckskin clothes and long hair and beard, he looked every bit the old prospector that he was. An 1885 publication characterized Sam as "a warm-hearted pioneer, whose latch-string always hangs out for the virtuous wayfarer."[1] At his funeral, forty carriages followed Sam's casket to Union Cemetery. The Livingstons' farm was obliterated in 1930–33 to create the Glenmore Reservoir, but part of their old 1883 farmhouse— where several of their fourteen children grew up—is preserved in Calgary's Heritage Park. The sandstone base of Sam's tombstone is original, but the honed sandstone obelisk, adorned by the Masonic emblem, is a replica. The original is in the churchyard at Heritage Park.

2. PRINCE, EMMA HOWSE
circa 1855–1902, 28-7-B;

PRINCE, ROSA DOUGLAS
circa 1852–1907, 28-7-B;

PRINCE, EMILY WHITLOCK
circa 1861–1944, 29-7-B

Pioneer industrialist Peter Prince (1836–1925) was a Quebec-born millwright who moved from Eau Claire, Wisconsin in 1886 to set up and manage Calgary's Eau Claire and Bow River Lumber Company. The city's Eau Claire district owes its name to Prince's enterprise, and a logging channel on the riverfront mill site turned a point bar into what is now Prince's Island Park. In 1894, Prince built a magnificent three-storey house based on plans published in *Scientific American*. Here he lived with his four wives: Marguerite Corogan, who died of diabetes in 1898; Emma Howse, an invalid who died of tuberculosis in 1902; Rosa Douglas, who died of cancer in 1907; and Emily Whitlock, a widow whom he married in 1909, and who outlived him. In 1967, the mansion in which each of them lived—and most of them died—was moved to Heritage Park. Peter and Marguerite are buried in nearby St. Mary's Roman Catholic Cemetery. Emma, Rosa, and Emily are buried together in this family plot. A white granite monument marks only Emma and Rosa's graves. The base of the monument resembles a cairn of stones; above the cairn, two intersecting logs form a Latin cross representing the Tree of Life.

3. Ross, Alexander J.
circa 1851–1894, 14-5-B

On November 7, 1885, photographer Alexander Ross took what is arguably the most famous picture in Canadian history. While railway workers and officials observe, Lord Strathcona drives the last spike in the CPR. The following year Ross settled in Calgary, where he maintained a studio, but also took up ranching. Ross' sandstone marker is badly eroded, leaving the epitaph barely legible. Atop the sandstone base is a small, jagged piece of Ross' sandstone obelisk.

4. Salterio, Joseph
1860–1892, 13-1-B

From 1888 until his death four years later, Halifax-born Joseph Salterio owned the Grand Central Hotel on Atlantic Avenue,

Thirteen-year-old Fred Collings (circa 1882–95) was killed accidentally while he and a friend were playing with guns. This is an excellent example of an anchor carved in relief, symbolizing hope and Christian faith. (P1)

which had survived the great fire of 1886 that destroyed a large portion of town. In 1892, during Salterio's ownership, Frank Hamilton and Harry Longabaugh, an American outlaw better known as the Sundance Kid, took over the hotel's saloon, but their partnership was short-lived. When Hamilton tried to cheat Sundance, according to one account, the Kid leaped over the bar "and before his feet hit the floor his gun barrel was jammed in his partner's middle."[2] The debt was paid, but Sundance soon returned to the United States. Salterio died only months later, at the age of thirty-two. Salterio's obelisk monument is made from sandstone; erosion has rendered it nearly illegible. His grand-nephew renewed the epitaph with a brass plaque placed at the rear.

5. Macleod, James Farquharson
1836–1894, 16-1-B (see photo, p. 30)

Atop the crest in one of the oldest sections of Union Cemetery, within sight of Macleod Trail, rests the man to whom Calgary owes its name—Colonel James F. Macleod. Born in 1836 on the Isle of Skye, Scotland, young Macleod immigrated with his family to Canada in 1854 and began his first career as a lawyer in 1860. He soon joined the militia and served as a brigade major in the 1870 Red River Rebellion. When the NWMP was formed in 1873, Macleod signed on and was quickly promoted to assistant commissioner. He led the force on its great trek across the prairies in 1874, and set up his headquarters at Fort Macleod. Macleod set about eradicating the illicit whisky trade, enforcing Canadian law and order, and negotiating with leaders of the Aboriginal peoples. His reputation for fairness earned their respect, and in 1877 Macleod successfully negotiated Treaty No. 7, which opened southern Alberta to non-native settlers, allowed the CPR to cross the prairies, and paved the way for a small NWMP fort to

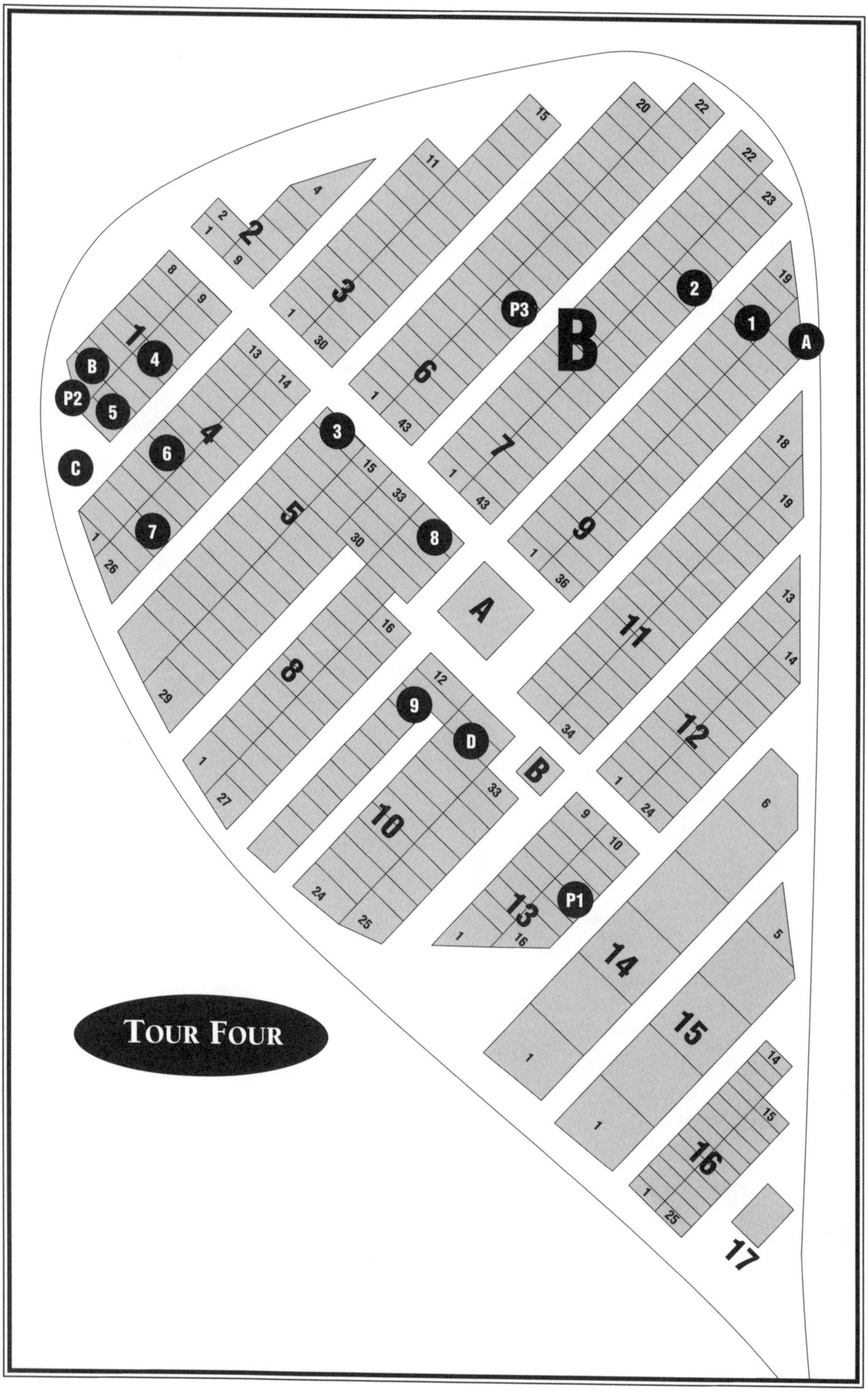
Tour Four
A
B
1
2
3
4
5
6
7
8
9
10
11
12
13
14
15
16
17
P1
P2
P3
C
D

MAP NOTES

◆ Section B contains the highest proportion of graves moved from Shaganappi Cemetery. As a result, many of the tombstones give death dates that predate Union Cemetery itself.

NOTES

A. Together with the nearby graves of SAMUEL HENRY HARKWOOD LIVINGSTON and Peter Prince's wives, Bernt J. Thorpe (1855–1931) rounds out Union Cemetery's "Heritage Park" corner. Originally from Norway, Thorpe came to Calgary in 1886 and became millwright for the Eau Claire & Bow River Lumber Company—which was managed by Peter Prince. Both the Thorpe and Prince houses have been moved to within sight of each other at Calgary's Heritage Park Historic Village. Samuel Livingston's house is also at Heritage Park.

B. The only flag in Union Cemetery is the Union Jack, which is raised above Colonel JAMES FARQUHARSON MACLEOD's grave. It was the flag under which he served as soldier, NWMP Commissioner, treaty negotiator, legislator, and judge.

C. From this spot are visible the graves of three sisters who witnessed the Red River Rebellion in 1869–70. Mary Drever is buried with her husband JAMES FARQUHARSON MACLEOD; Jean Drever is with her husband WILLIAM CYPRIAN PINKHAM; and Christiana lies buried with her husband, JOHN PASCOE JERMY JEPHSON.

D. William Nimmons (1824–1919) was one of forty-nine people taken prisoner in 1869 by Louis Riel's provisional government in Manitoba. He escaped before the Red River

Rebellion turned violent. In 1882, Nimmons paid eight dollars per acre for a ranch that he later subdivided as the present Bankview neighbourhood. The sandstone quarry that he started on his property provided stone for many early Calgary buildings. His brick ranch house still stands at 1827 - 14th Street SW.

develop into the City of Calgary. Macleod's influence on Calgary's development was even more direct. In 1875 he had dispatched F Troop, commanded by Inspector Ephrem Brisebois, to establish a post on the Bow River. Without authorization, the unpopular inspector styled the new post Fort Brisebois. On Macleod's recommendation, the Bow Fort (as it was officially known) was renamed Fort Calgary, after Calgary House in his native Scotland. Macleod resigned in 1876 to become a judge, but returned to the NWMP as commissioner from 1877 to 1880. He served as a judge of the Supreme Court of the Northwest Territories from 1887 until his death in Calgary in 1894. As a jurist, Macleod held a seat on the territorial council in Regina. He was a reluctant politician. "We had two meetings of the Council today," he once wrote, "but did not get thro[ugh] very much. Such an amount of twaddle was talked."[3] In 1876 he married Mary Isabella Drever (1852–1933). For all his service, Colonel Macleod died poor, reportedly leaving "a wife, five children and eight dollars."[4] His grave and original tombstone had deteriorated by the mid-1920s, when the present grey granite monument was placed.

6. PINKHAM, WILLIAM CYPRIAN
1844–1928, 6-4-B

The Right Reverend Pinkham, Calgary's first Anglican bishop, was born in Newfoundland. Ordained in 1869, Pinkham later became Archdeacon of Manitoba and then served concurrently as Bishop of Saskatchewan (1887–1903) and Bishop of Calgary (1888–1926). The Pinkhams' palatial residence on 4th Avenue West proved too large and was later converted into a private hotel, Braemar Lodge (see ANNIE ELIZABETH MOLLISON). His wife Jean (1849–1940) was a driving force in establishing the Calgary General Hospital in 1890.

7. BRADEN, THOMAS B.
1851–1904, 24-4-B

In the summer of 1883, a former Ontario school teacher and partisan Liberal arrived in the tent and shack settlement of Calgary in advance of the railway, intent on starting a newspaper. Braden collected one hundred subscriptions the day he arrived, and on August 31, 1883, he and partner Andrew Moorhead Armour launched the *Calgary Herald, Mining and Ranche Review and General Advertiser*. Braden sold his interest in the *Herald* and in 1885 he launched the *Calgary Tribune and Bow River District Advertiser*, later renamed the *Albertan*. Braden returned to the *Herald* in 1894 but quit shortly before his death. "Very few people here are acquainted with a Calgary without T.B. Braden," the *Albertan* eulogized. "It may be said that there has been no Calgary without T.B. Braden."[5] Braden's name has nearly worn off from the badly eroded sandstone monument he shares with sister Emma and brother George. The settling of the grave has caused the stone to lean.

8. ROBERTSON, ANGUS
1856–1890, 15-8-B

In September 1890, the late Angus Robertson—Calgary's original Presbyterian minister—became the first person buried in Union Cemetery. Born near Guelph, Ontario, and ordained in Winnipeg, the young minister arrived in Calgary in June 1883—two months ahead of the CPR. He established Knox Presbyterian Church (known as Knox United Church after the church union of 1925). In 1890, the thirty-four-year-old minister contracted typhoid and died in Medicine Hat. His body was brought to Calgary for burial. "This was the first interment in the new cemetery," noted the *Calgary Tribune*, "and the plot selected was on a beautiful knoll on the top of the hill."[6] However, Robertson's present grave may not have been his original one. At the time of his death, the town

Colonel James F. Macleod's grave and headstone were renewed in 1925 during the golden jubilee anniversary of Fort Calgary's establishment. (P2)

The Leeson family plot has the sole remaining example of intact iron fencing. It includes a white bronze obelisk marker, with a name plate cast separately. Apocryphally, this type of monument was used to hide liquor for later retrieval. (P3)

had set aside a "temporary" burial ground while Union Cemetery was being laid out. It seems possible that Robertson, along with others buried in 1890 and 1891, were exhumed and reinterred after the cemetery plan was adopted. A century after his death, the Presbytery of Calgary/Macleod placed a brass plaque on the badly eroded sandstone monument to renew Robertson's illegible epitaph. A second plaque memorializes his widow Susan (1857–1916), who died returning from China and was buried at sea.

9. KING, GEORGE CLIFT
1848–1935, 10-10-B

Calgary's "first citizen," Corporal George Clift King of the NWMP, was the first Mountie to set foot on the future site of Fort Calgary in 1875. Born in England, King immigrated to Canada in 1874 and joined the newly formed NWMP. He was assigned to F Troop, under the command of Inspector Ephrem Brisebois, which established and garrisoned Fort Calgary. King retired from the force before his thirtieth birthday and became the local manager for I.G. Baker & Co., a Montana-based mercantile firm that built the original Fort Calgary under government

contract. He was elected mayor in 1886, shortly before the devastating fire that led to Calgary's reconstruction as the Sandstone City. Defeated in 1888, King later served several terms as an alderman. In 1934 King was awarded the OBE for his thirty-six years as Calgary's postmaster (1885–1921). In commemoration of Fort Calgary's 125th anniversary in 2000, an oval-topped grey granite tablet was placed on King's previously unmarked grave. Louise King, his wife, is buried in St. Mary's Roman Catholic Cemetery.

Notes

1. *Calgary, Alberta, Canada*, compiled and edited by Burns & Elliott ([Calgary]: Glenbow Alberta Institute / McClelland and Stewart West, 1974), 77

2. Vicky Kelly, "Butch and the Kid," *Glenbow* 3, no. 6 (November 1970): 4.

3. Glenbow Archives, James Farquharson Macleod Family fonds, M776/14a.

4. Lawrie Knight-Steinbach, *Union Cemetery Interpretive Tour* (Calgary: The City of Calgary Heritage Advisory Board, [1994?]), 26.

5. *Albertan*, 24 August 1904.

6. *Calgary Tribune*, 3 September 1890.

TOUR FIVE

Sections C and D

JEPHSON, JOHN PASCOE JERMY
died 1923, 3-1-C

In its relentless growth, the City of Calgary has absorbed a series of neighbouring villages and towns, among them Crescent Heights, Forest Lawn, Bowness, and Montgomery. The first was Rouleauville, a largely Roman Catholic settlement founded south of what is now 17th Avenue SW, and incorporated as a village in 1899. Its first overseer (a position equivalent to mayor or reeve) was Cambridge-educated lawyer J. P. J. Jephson, who had arrived in Calgary in 1886. English-born and Protestant, Jephson became a prominent citizen in Rouleauville, a community dominated by Roman Catholics of French and Irish descent. Calgary grew faster than its southern neighbour and in 1907 the village was absorbed as the residential district of Mission. Jephson was married to Christiana Drever, who had survived the Red River Rebellion in 1870 and gave evidence at Louis Riel's trial that year. The Jephsons' tombstone is a rustic grey granite Latin cross, resting on a grey granite pedestal base.

2. MCKENZIE, JAMES A.
1842–1919, 25-4-C

In the late 1860s and early 1870s, a group of Irish-Americans known as the Fenians launched a series of ineffective raids on Canada, which they proposed to capture and ransom for Irish independence. Among the officers they faced in a raid on Megantic County, Quebec, was James A. McKenzie of the 55th Infantry. Decorated

for his service, McKenzie left his native Quebec in 1887 for Calgary, Northwest Territories, where he had one last act of bravery ahead of him. In 1895, McKenzie was foreman of construction on the Bow Marsh Bridge, which led to the present day Hillhurst district. A worker named Adolph Kettleson fell from the unfinished bridge, struck his head, plunged into the river, and was swept away by the current. McKenzie leapt into the river and saved Kettleson from a watery grave. He received a medal

The Carson family's white granite monument includes a sculpted Holy Bible and a Maltese cross. (P1)

from the Royal Canadian Humane Society for his heroism. McKenzie served four terms on city council beginning in 1895. He resigned in 1904 over a lot-selling controversy. McKenzie's headstone is a mahogany granite screen with floral relief and checks in the corners.

3. COOPER, HARRY A.
1857–1899, 20-8-C

Although he was not listed in the *Guinness Book of World Records*, Yorkshire-born Harry Cooper stood eight feet, six inches tall, and was rumoured to be the tallest man in the world. He could light his pipe from gas-lit street lamps. When a circus passed through Brotton, where Cooper was working as an iron miner, his life took an unexpected turn. He was "discovered," joined the circus, and toured Britain as the Yorkshire Giant. He later moved to Philadelphia and toured North America, known variously as Sir Henry Alexander Cooper and Colonel H. A. Cooper, but billed as the English Giant. In August 1899, Cooper came to Calgary with the Walter Main Circus, but succumbed to illness and died in the Calgary General Hospital before the circus performed. (As might be expected, the show did go on.) Cooper was buried by the Odd Fellows and the Knights of Pythias, of which he was a member. His unmarked grave, part of a block of Odd Fellows plots, lies immediately south of Alfred John Cameron.

4. BOWDEN, ELIZABETH JANE
1858–1941, (13-14)-10-C

The old CPR station on 9th Avenue was probably Elizabeth Bowden's introduction to Calgary when she and her husband Elijah arrived in 1898. Widowed in 1900, the Ottawa-born woman became the CPR "matron," operating the station's restaurant for thirty-eight years. "How well I remember," recalled LEISHMAN MCNEILL,

chronicler of early Calgary, "seeing Mrs. Bowden out on the platform, ringing the dinner bell advertising a good meal for a cost of only about 35c."[1] A white marble Latin cross marks the Bowdens' graves.

5. WILSON, JAMES EDGAR
1857–1920, 11-10-C

After the great fire of 1886, which destroyed a wide swath of downtown Calgary, town council reorganized the volunteer fire brigade and built a brick fire hall on McIntyre (now 7th) Avenue. So pleased were the civic fathers with the new edifice—a much superior building to the wooden town hall—that they promptly moved in. The fire brigade, frustrated at the intrusion, sold their furniture and resigned en masse. Eventually the town fathers bowed to public pressure, moved back to their own building, and reconstituted the fire brigade in the summer of 1889. That's when James E. Wilson, a carpenter from Norfolk, Ontario, joined the brigade. He rose quickly through the ranks and was elected fire chief in 1893. Wilson resigned in 1896 to become Calgary's first paid fire engineer, and went on to serve as building inspector, foreman over all public works, and, from 1906 to 1912, superintendent of Waterworks. During his tenure, the City replaced the inadequate, privately built waterworks system it had acquired in 1900 with a $340,000, gravity-fed system that remained in use until 1933, when it was replaced by the Glenmore dam and reservoir. When Wilson died, nearly one hundred members of the old volunteer brigade—including his successor, JAMES "CAPPY" SMART—marched with his remains from the fire hall to the undertaker. An obelisk is evidently missing from Wilson's small grey marble monument; the only remaining inscription is his family's name.

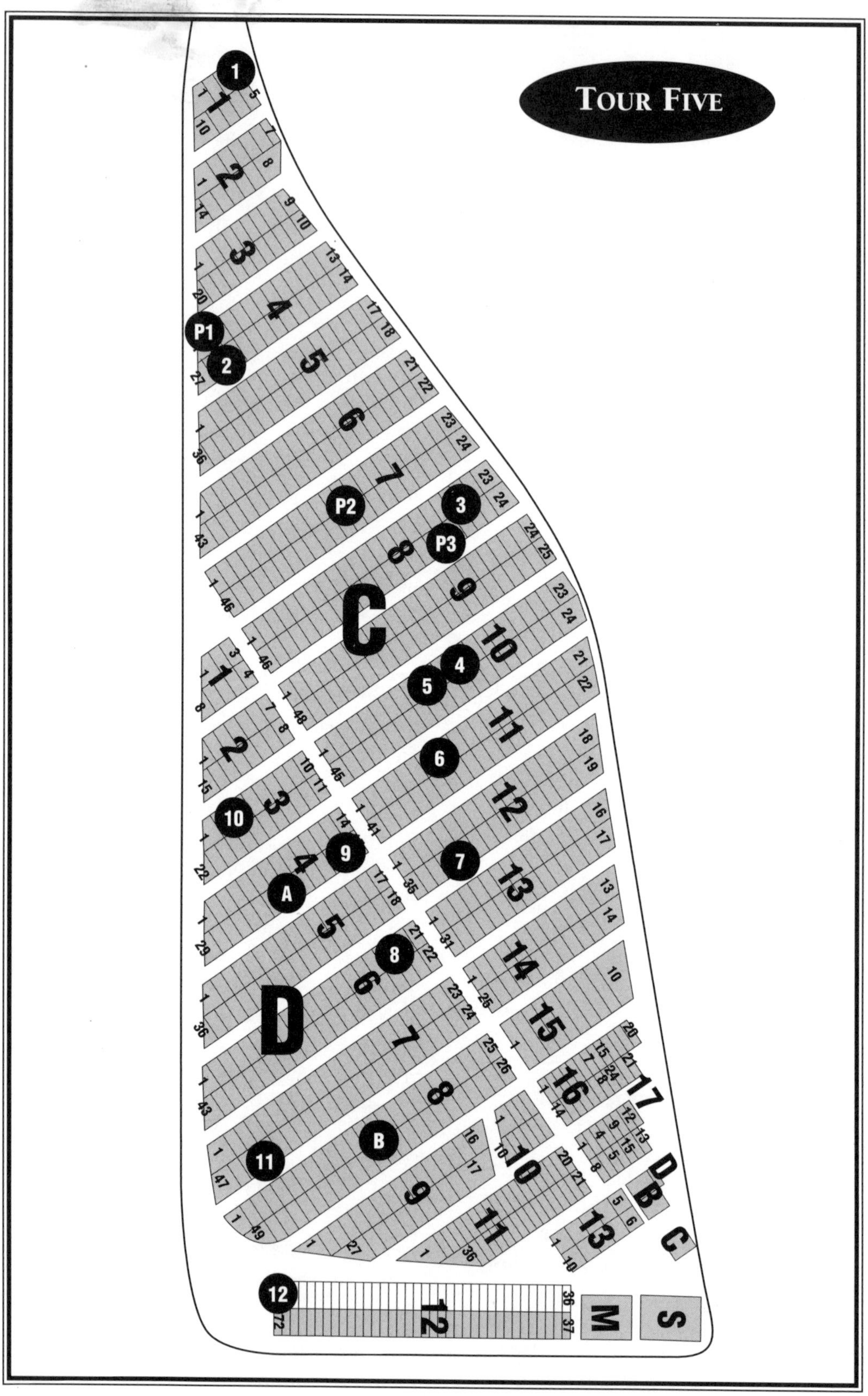
Tour Five
C
D
M
S

MAP NOTES

◆ Sections C and D share the same "island", and the only rationale for separating them into separate sections is the pathway that runs between the two.

◆ The first two caretakers of Union Cemetery, Robert L. Barker (circa 1861–1939) and James H. Galloway (1861–1941), are buried in Section C.

◆ At least four hotel-keepers are buried in Section C: Hugh S. McLeod (1860–1913), who owned the Grand Central Hotel; Fred Adams (1864–1946), of the Victoria and Alexandra hotels; Robert C. Thomas (1862–1950), the Royal and Wales hotels; and Charles Traunweiser (1873–1954), the Commercial, Yale, and Carlton hotels.

NOTES

A. James Moseley (1818–1908) was a veteran of the 1837 Upper Canada Rebellion. He claimed to have been the man who first brought news of William Lyon Mackenzie's rebellion to Sheriff Jarvis of Toronto.

B. Two rows in Section D were granted to the NWMP in the 1890s for mounted police burials. Constable Francis Walter Davies, who was murdered in 1913, is buried here. (See JOHN C. FISK for the tale of Davies' dog.) The RCMP Veterans Association looks after these graves.

6. SIMPSON, ARTHUR
circa 1878–1902, 8-11-C

The Atlantic Hotel was known as one of Calgary's roughest bars long before Arthur Simpson's violent death cemented its reputation as "the Bucket of Blood." Built in 1890 as Temperance House, the hotel's character changed radically after Prohibition ended in 1892. Its location—now the site of the Salvation Army's Centre of Hope—positioned the Atlantic as the Last Chance Saloon for anyone leaving Calgary to the east or by the old Macleod Trail. For anyone arriving from the opposite direction, it became the First Chance Saloon. Beatings, brawls, and robberies were a regular occurrence at the Atlantic, and it was here on March 16, 1902 that Simpson, an English-born tentmaker, interfered in a scuffle that ended his life. Simpson was in the dining room that Sunday evening when a fight broke out between the three partners who ran the Atlantic Stables next door. A crowd of onlookers—with Simpson at the front—gathered around them. One of the partners was former special constable George Scoughton, who later testified he had been drinking heavily. Scoughton was evidently angered by a comment from the crowd, threw a punch at Simpson, and the fight was on. It lasted only a minute. Just as Simpson appeared victorious, two gunshots rang out. Simpson, mortally wounded, staggered toward hotel owner Roy Mackenzie and said, "Well, Mac, I'm done for."[2] At Scoughton's trial, witness Arthur Cato testified he saw Scoughton fire a gun. Scoughton was found guilty of manslaughter and sentenced to ten years in prison. Simpson is buried in an unmarked grave immediately south of William John Hunter.

Eugene Phelps was fatally injured in a 1901 railway accident, and his Masonic brethren took care of his funeral. The Masonic symbol, the square and calipers, reflects his membership in that organization. (P2)

7. TRAUNWEISER, EDNA
died 1918, 31-12-C

In the dying days of World War I, a world-wide epidemic of Spanish influenza killed more people than had perished in the conflict. Citizen volunteers assisted medical professionals in caring for the sick and the dying. According to her *Herald* obituary, Edna Traunweiser "had a strong desire to take some active part in the care of stricken soldiers"[3] after her brother George had been killed in action. Edna, who already had some nursing training, volunteered at the Sarcee Camp hospital. She succumbed to influenza after only a week, and died of double pneumonia. Edna was buried on November 11, 1918—the last day of the war. Her unmarked grave is just east of Frederick D. Adams.

8. JONES, ALICE TODD
1877–1911, 19-6-D

In 1912, the *Canadian Alpine Journal* eulogized the late Allie Jones as "a devoted supporter of the [Canadian Alpine] Club and its ideals, an enthusiastic lover of Nature as seen in the mountain wilds, and a charming and sympathetic comrade around the camp fire."[4] She was one of the first woman mountain climbers in Canada, and the first married woman to climb Mt. Vice-President. Born in Walkerton, Ontario, Allie Todd married Calgary lawyer, Boer War veteran, and mountaineer Stanley Livingstone Jones in 1905. Major Jones is buried in France, where he died in 1916 as a German prisoner of war. His name is perpetuated through Stanley Jones Elementary School in northeast Calgary. Because of its proximity to the school, the old Calgary Municipal Airport (in use from 1929–39) was commonly known as the Stanley Jones Airport. A diminutive grey marble western slant marker identifies her grave.

9. BRUMBY, ERNEST ARTHUR
circa 1884–1909, 16-4-D

Typhoid fever, frequently caused by contaminated well water, was a common and sometimes fatal occurrence in early twentieth-century Calgary. Most victims were in their twenties, and young Ernest Brumby, a twenty-six-year-old bookkeeper originally from England, fit the profile. Brumby moved to Calgary from Toronto in 1908, found work with an insurance firm, and joined the Church of the Redeemer, where he taught Sunday school and sang in the choir. He lay ill for three weeks before typhoid claimed his life. Brumby's epitaph is one of the few in Union Cemetery that gives cause of death. A severe typhoid epidemic in 1910 led in part to the conversion of the old Calgary General Hospital in Victoria Park into an isolation hospital.

The preserved sandstone ruins of the hospital still stand on 12th Avenue SE. Lichen covers the sandstone base of Brumby's grey marble-shouldered tablet.

10. Hextall, John
circa 1861–1914, 3-3-D

Though his dream of creating "the suburb perfect" was shattered, lawyer John Hextall bequeathed a legacy that generations of Calgarians have enjoyed: Bowness Park. Hextall and his family left England in 1908, ostensibly to take up a ranching life. He was taken with the lovely Bowness Ranche, on the banks of the Bow River upstream from Calgary. But in the context of Calgary's real estate boom, Hextall saw development potential rather than idyllic

Like other fraternal societies, the International Order of Odd Fellows purchased contiguous plots for use by their members. In 1906, the IOOF placed a red granite pedestal topped with an urn to mark this area as an Odd Fellows section. (P3)

beauty. He paid over two hundred thousand dollars for the land, which he subdivided as Bowness Park Estates, and spent hundreds of thousands more to build a bridge, an electrical plant, a water tower, and a golf course and clubhouse. Hextall envisioned a luxury enclave, where well-to-do Englishmen would build palatial homes on one- or two-acre lots. He built his own mansion there, as well as four other houses to demonstrate Bowness' potential. For his distant suburb to succeed, Hextall needed a streetcar line connecting Bowness with Calgary. In 1911 he donated the bridge and two islands to the City in exchange for a streetcar line. But "the suburb perfect" was stillborn. Within two years Calgary's boom turned bust, Hextall died, and World War I began. The water tower was condemned after a typhoid outbreak, and lightning destroyed the power plant. Hextall's mansion, later used as Wood's Christian Home for homeless children, was demolished in 1975. Hextall's real legacy is Bowness Park, which the City developed on the islands he donated. For decades, the Bowness streetcar crossed empty prairie to reach the park, which became a weekend haven for Calgarians. Bowness became a town in 1958 and was annexed to Calgary in 1964. A white marble Latin cross marks Hextall's grave.

11. Doll, Louis Henry
1867–1961, 44-7-D

From 1889 to 1908, Ontario-born Louis H. Doll operated a landmark jewellery and watchmaking business on Stephen Avenue. At the height of his success in 1907, Doll built his "Diamond Palace", a three-storey brick and sandstone showcase described as "the largest and most handsome jewelry house west of Toronto."[5] Within a year, however, Doll's jewellery career came to an end. Deeply affected by the untimely death of his young daughter Florence, Doll lost all interest in his business and sold it to a former apprentice, David E. Black, who is also buried in Section D (11-13-D). Evidently Doll became a broken man. He was convicted in 1918 of uttering forged cheques, and in 1921 he was committed to the mental institution at Ponoka. Though his death in 1961 went unnoticed in Calgary, Doll is not forgotten. The façade of his "Diamond Palace," incorporated into the convention centre in 2000, still bears the name "L.H. Doll." Doll, his wife Mary, and their daughter Florence share a black granite western slant marker, seen from the rear from this direction.

12. TOWSE, CHARLES
1885–1915, 1-12-D;

SWINDELLS, MAY
1890–1915, 2-12-D

On an April night in 1915, thirty-year-old Charles Towse walked arm in arm with his fiancée, twenty-five-year-old May Swindells, to the Prospect Avenue home where she boarded. Charles was from Scotland, May from England, and neither had relatives in the city. Charles worked for the Robin Hood Milling Company and had recently bought a house on the North Hill; the couple was to be married in a month's time. Only blocks from May's house they were hit by a single bolt of lightning and both killed. Their bodies were found the following morning, lying in the middle of Prospect Avenue near 10th Street West. The couple lies side by side in unmarked graves. Charles is next to a park bench; May is buried beside him. The next grave to the north is Emily, wife of Thomas Hunt.

Notes

1. Leishman McNeill, *The Calgary Herald's Tales of the Old Town* (Calgary: Calgary Herald, [1966]), 24.
2. *Albertan and the Alberta Tribune*, 18 March 1902.
3. *Calgary Daily Herald*, 12 November 1918.
4. *Canadian Alpine Journal* vol. 4, (1912), 136.
5. Harry Hume, *Prosperous Calgary* ([Calgary]: Calgary Daily Herald, 1908).

Section L

1. ADAMS, SAMUEL HUNTER
1878–1975, 2-11B-L

In 1906, Ontario-born schoolteacher Sam Adams arrived in Calgary with only forty-five dollars to his name. He immediately spent twenty dollars on curling stones, leaving only twenty-five dollars to establish himself in his new city. Adams articled in law and was called to the bar in 1909. He served five consecutive terms on city council before defeating his friend, fellow alderman Isaac Ruttle, for the mayor's chair in 1920. The contest was reportedly so civil that Ruttle drove Adams—who had no car—to campaign meetings. During his term as mayor (1921–23), Adams officially opened the Capitol and Palace theatres and gave the inaugural speech on Calgary's

first radio station, CHCB. In 1922, Adams planted the first of many trees along Memorial Drive in memory of the fallen soldiers of World War I. During an unemployment crisis that year, in which he took a harsh attitude towards unemployed men, Adams received a bomb threat. A week later someone hurled a brick through his office window. The next day, *Calgary Herald* reporter Chief Buffalo Child Long Lance pulled a stunt that ended his journalistic career. In disguise, Long Lance entered the mayor's office—crowded with department heads, commissioners, and reporters—with a convincing phony bomb. Most ran from the room, but one of the commissioners broke through a window and fell twelve feet to the ground. The incident became national news. Adams

Dr. Thomas H. Quirk, a dentist killed in a freak auto accident, is buried in Union Cemetery's only remaining mausoleum. (P1)

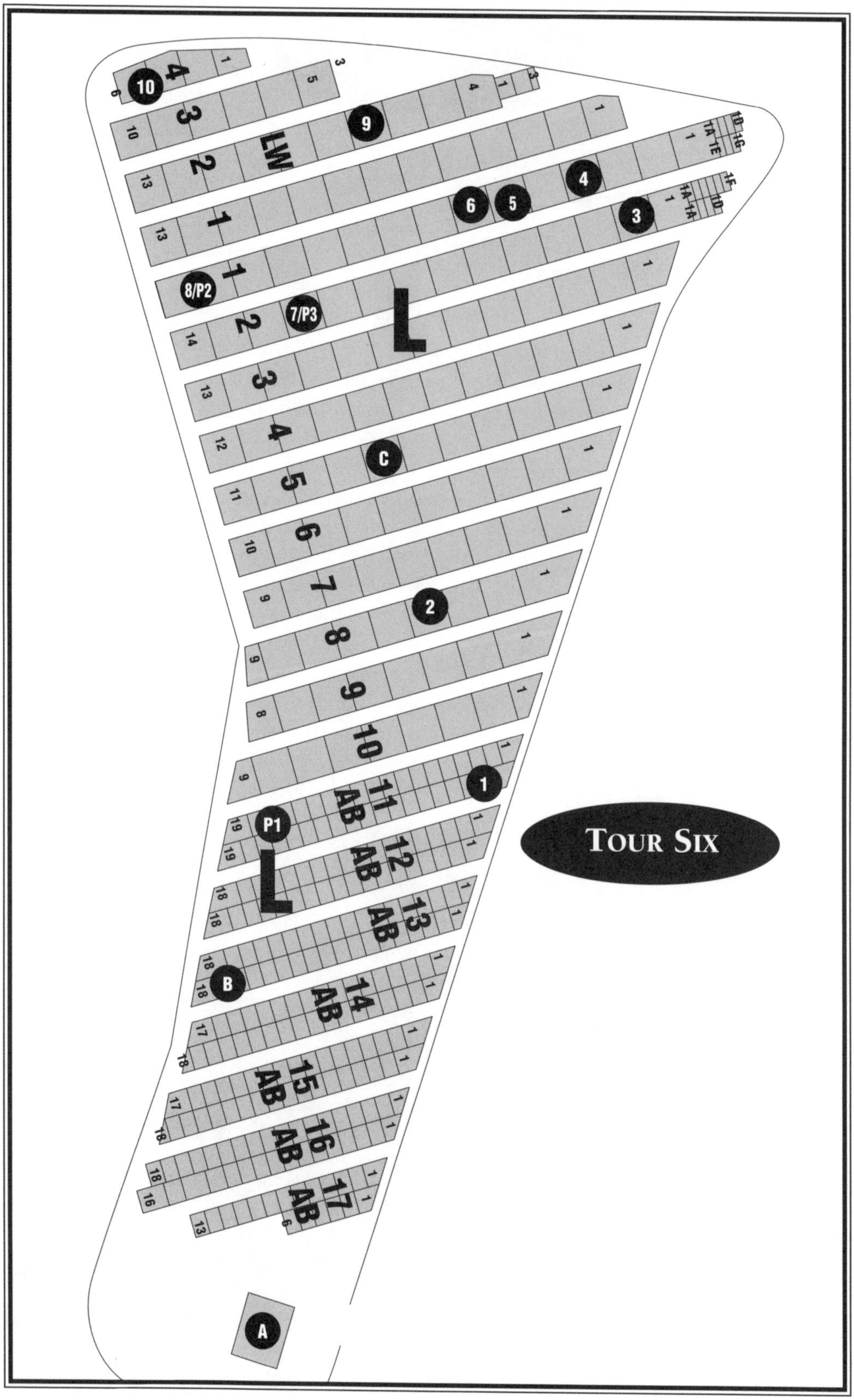
TOUR SIX
LW
L
8/P2
7/P3
P1
A
B
C

MAP NOTES

◆ Large family plots on the west side of Section L can accommodate up to ten burials.

◆ Six former mayors of Calgary are buried in Section L: GEORGE MURDOCH (1884–86); James Delamere Lafferty (1890–91); James Reilly (1891–92, 1899–1900); Thomas Underwood (1902–04); REUBEN RUPERT JAMIESON (1909–11); and SAMUEL H. ADAMS (1921–23). Visitors should stay on the path until they find a level approach, then walk to Samuel Adams' grave.

NOTES

A. Built in 1899, the brick caretaker's cottage at the cemetery entrance along Macleod Trail (now Spiller Road) was later covered in stucco. James Galloway's former residence has long served as the cemetery office, workshop and garage.

B. Of all the Calgarians lost on the *Empress of Ireland* in 1914, Arthur Edward Stillman was the best-known. Thousands attended the funeral of the young company executive and president of the Baptist Young People's Society. A highly visible black granite monument, topped by a roll, identifies his grave.

C. The International Typographical Union monument was erected by Calgary Typographical Union No. 440, to the memory of members who died in the Great War of 1914–18. ITU members are buried in the adjacent plots.

returned to his law practice in 1922, and retired to British Columbia in 1956. He died during Calgary's first centennial year in 1975. Adams' memorial is a bronze plaque on a concrete base.

2. MURDOCH, GEORGE
1850–1910, 4-8-L

Calgary's first mayor was born in Paisley, Scotland, but grew up in Saint John, New Brunswick, where his family settled in 1854. In 1883 Murdoch moved to Calgary and opened a harness shop; later he built the Park Hotel. Murdoch quickly became active in the unincorporated community of some four hundred people. He joined the civic committee that sought town incorporation, and was elected as the town's first mayor in December 1884. Murdoch was re-elected in 1885, defeating James Reilly (who is buried in 3-10-L, within sight of Murdoch's grave). However, magistrate JEREMIAH TRAVIS accused Murdoch and his slate of candidates with corruption and of being part of a "Whisky Ring." Travis disqualified their election and declared Reilly and his slate the victors. Murdoch and his group refused to resign and kept the books and seal. For ten months, Calgary went ungoverned. Finally the unpopular Travis was removed from the bench and a new election was called. Murdoch ran again, but was defeated by GEORGE CLIFT KING. History recognizes Murdoch, not Reilly, as mayor in 1886. The Shriners' emblem appears on Murdoch's apex-topped, blue pearl granite screen.

3. WALSH, WILLIAM LEGH
1857–1938, 2-2-L

In his nineteen years on the bench of the Supreme Court of Alberta, Justice William L. Walsh earned a reputation for fairness and an "unflinching sense of justice." Fate handed Walsh more than his share of capital cases, resulting in eighteen executions and the nickname "the Hanging Judge."

In one case, Walsh tried a man accused of two murders, and through a legal quirk was forced to impose two death sentences. His most famous case took place during Prohibition, when bootlegger Emilio Picariello and his accomplice Florence Lassandro were tried and executed for murder in 1922. Born in Simcoe, Ontario, Walsh was the scion of a staunch Tory family, and both his father and grandfather had sat in Parliament. Walsh served three terms as mayor of Orangeville, Ontario, and nearly won the mayoralty of Dawson City, Yukon Territory, in 1904. While living in Dawson from 1900 to 1904, Walsh became the lawyer for Skookum Jim, one of the three original prospectors whose 1896 discovery at Bonanza Creek had sparked the Klondike Gold Rush. Walsh moved to Calgary in 1904 and became the founding president of the Alberta Conservative Association the following year. In 1931 Prime Minister R. B. Bennett appointed him to a five-year term as Lieutenant-Governor of Alberta. Walsh proved a widely popular public figure, known to friends and admirers as "Daddy." He died in Victoria, where he had retired in 1938. Bronze pillow markers identify those buried in the Walsh family plot.

Memorial to Douglas Edgar Wait (1918–22), four-year-old son of Edgar A. Wait. It is an Italian statue, carved from white marble, depicting a winged cherub placing a wreath on a Latin cross. The epitaph reads: *SLEEP ON SWEET BABE / AND TAKE THY REST / GOD CALLED THEE HOME / HE THOUGHT IT BEST.* (P2)

4. DICK, ALBERT ADRIAN
1880–1970, 4-1-L;

DICK, VERA
1894–1973, 4-1-L

A seventeen-year-old-girl, in the company of a wealthy, thirty-something man, travels first class aboard the world's largest and most luxurious ocean vessel. She dines with Thomas Andrews, the ship's designer, and wears a heart-shaped gem that her beau has given her. After the ship's fated collision with an iceberg, she stands on the open deck and breathes in the cold, bracing air. She initially resists getting in the lifeboat if it means leaving behind the man

she loves. Ultimately, she is rescued, and arrives in New York aboard the *Carpathia*. This young woman is not Rose DeWitt Bukater, the fictional heroine of James Cameron's 1998 film *Titanic*. She is Vera Dick, the young bride of wealthy Calgary businessman Bert Dick. Unlike Rose, who despised her fiancé Cal, Vera was devoted to the man who gave her the gem—in her case, a ruby. And unlike Rose, Vera lost her jewel when the *Titanic* went down. *Titanic* historian Wyn Craig Wade has identified Vera as the source of the myth that the band played "Nearer My God To Thee" as the ship was sinking. Like Vera, Bert survived and returned to Calgary. "The [life]boat we came on was one of the last to leave," Vera told a reporter. "There was plenty of room in it, so I simply insisted on my husband getting in with me, and why not, pray?"[1] Nonetheless, Bert probably faced disapproval for the rest of his life from those who thought only women and children should have been in the lifeboats. A single granite marker identifies Bert and Vera's grave.

5. JAMIESON, REUBEN RUPERT
1856–1911, 6-1-L;

JAMIESON, ALICE
1860–1949, 6-1-L

Born in Westover, Ontario, R. R. Jamieson studied telegraphy before moving to the United States in 1878 to work for a series of American railroad companies. There he met New York-born Alice Jane Jukes, whom he married in 1882. The following year they moved to Canada, where R. R. went to work for the CPR. Around 1903 he was transferred to Calgary as general superintendent of its western division. R. R. resigned after being transferred to Winnipeg, returned to Calgary, and ran successfully for mayor. During his tenure (1909–11), the waterworks system was replaced and the Calgary Municipal Railway inaugurated. R. R. lost his bid to become a city commissioner in the 1910 election and declared that municipal politics "had seen the last of him." He died less than six months later.

Alice Jamieson was a leading advocate for women's interests, and a founder and president of the Calgary Local Council of Women, an organization that helped achieve women's suffrage in Alberta in 1916. She was appointed judge of the juvenile court in 1913, and became the first woman in the British Empire to

hold such a position. Three years later she was appointed police magistrate in the women's court, becoming Canada's second female police magistrate after Edmonton's Emily Murphy. Her appointment aroused opposition from the male establishment—including Calgary lawyer JOHN MCKINLEY CAMERON, who appealed a female client's 1917 conviction on the grounds that Alice's appointment had been unconstitutional. The appeal reached the provincial supreme court, where Justice Charles Stuart (see Tour 3, Note B) confirmed that women could indeed be judges. Alice retired from the bench in 1932. The Jamiesons share an elaborately carved Canada rose granite tablet.

6. TRAVIS, JEREMIAH
1830–1911, 7-1-L

The very name Jeremiah Travis evokes the "wild west" that this Harvard-trained New Brunswick lawyer came to subdue. Until 1892 the Northwest Territories was legally a prohibition zone. Although Calgary was otherwise a law-abiding town, bootlegging and legal loopholes meant Calgary had dozens of wide-open saloons. In 1885 Jerry Travis was appointed as stipendiary magistrate, replacing Mayor GEORGE MURDOCH— a fellow citizen from Saint John, New Brunswick—in the post. There the similarity ended. The teetotaller Travis quickly identified a powerful "Whisky Ring" headed by none other than the mayor himself. The new magistrate acted quickly to apply the letter of the law. He jailed both Simon John Clarke, a saloonkeeper and one of Murdoch's town councillors, and *Calgary Herald* editor Hugh S. Cayley for a scathing editorial that amounted to contempt *out of* court. Sensing electoral corruption, Travis disallowed Murdoch's re-election in 1885 and attempted to install the losing candidate, James Reilly, as mayor. After a citizens' meeting to discuss the situation, one man remarked "that a

Funeral of Sir James Lougheed, November 8, 1925. (Glenbow Archives, NA-3232-20) (P3)

barrel should be filled with dynamite and placed under Judge Travis and blow him to hell."[2] Travis made many enemies, and orchestrated pressure removed him from office after only twenty months. Although he never returned to the bench, Travis remained in Calgary and made a considerable fortune in real estate. His initials stand in relief on the pediment of his blue granite tablet.

7. QUIRK, THOMAS HOPKINS
died 1912, 11-2-L (see photo p. 39)

Born in Nevada, Quirk was educated in dentistry at the University of California Dental College and moved to Calgary around 1907. Advertising "painless dentistry," by 1912 Quirk had established a successful practice, married, had two young sons, and had just built a beautiful new home in Elbow Park. While driving friends home from downtown on the night of October 1, 1912, Quirk was killed in a freak collision on 1st Street West. The automobile he was driving struck a horse-

drawn street-flushing cart; though the horse was only lightly injured, Quirk and one of his passengers were killed. Nellie Quirk built this white marble mausoleum—the only such structure remaining in Union Cemetery—for her late husband. The mausoleum was vandalized in 1991 and Quirk's skull was stolen. It was later recovered and the vandal was arrested.

8. LOUGHEED, SIR JAMES ALEXANDER
1854–1925, 14-1-L

A grey granite "Exedra" bench serves as a headstone for the family plot of the Lougheeds, Alberta's equivalent to the Kennedy political dynasty. Patriarch James A. Lougheed was born in Brampton, Ontario, and learned carpentry from his father before studying law at Osgoode Hall. Lougheed arrived in Calgary in 1883, ahead of the CPR, and soon became the railway syndicate's legal counsel. His law practice later included R. B. Bennett (prime minister from 1930 to 1935) as a partner.

Lougheed's land investments in downtown Calgary became enormously valuable, and among the office buildings he constructed were the Clarence, Douglas, Edgar, and Norman blocks, named for sons who are also buried here. (The historic Clarence and Norman blocks still stand on the Stephen Avenue Mall.) He was appointed to the Canadian Senate in 1889, and later served as Senate Conservative Leader and as a minister in the federal cabinet. Lougheed headed the Military Hospitals Commission during World War I, and for this service he was knighted in 1916. In 1884 he married Isabella Hardisty (1860–1936), daughter of the Hudson's Bay Company's chief factor for the Mackenzie district. As Lady Belle Lougheed, she became Calgary's most prominent society matron. The family's sandstone mansion still stands at 707 - 13th Avenue SW. One of the many pillow markers in this family plot belongs to Edgar Lougheed (1893–1951), whose son Peter served as premier of Alberta from 1971 to 1985.

9. MOODIE, MARION ELIZABETH
1867–1958, 7-2-L (West)

When she completed her training at the Calgary General Hospital in 1898, Marion Moodie became the first nurse to graduate in Alberta. Her training began at the original General, a converted two-storey house with bullet holes in the front door. One of her first patients was a man with cancer of the tongue. "Across from him," Moodie wrote in her diary, "was an Irishwoman with synovitis of the knee, who was an inveterate talker and used to make the most of any opportunity to get to talk to the tongueless man, until he besought us, by gestures, to pitch her through the window."[3] During World War I, Moodie served as matron of the Ogden Red Cross Military Convalescent Hospital. Her varied interests included botany, painting, and writing

poetry. Some of her botanical specimens went to the Smithsonian Institution and the Field Museum in Chicago. Her poetry was published under such titles as *Songs of the West* and *The Legend of Dryas*. Moodie left Calgary in 1920 but returned in 1951. She shares a grey granite tablet with other family members.

10. HARRADENCE, RODERICK RICHARD
1953–1986, 4-4-L (West)

"GREATER LOVE HATH NO / MAN THAN THIS, THAT A MAN / LAY DOWN HIS OWN LIFE / FOR HIS FRIENDS," reads the epitaph on Rod Harradence's black tombstone. On June 6, 1986, an Alberta Fish and Wildlife biologist and his pilot went missing in Kananaskis Country, where they had flown to assess wildlife conditions on Mount Allan in advance of the 1988 Olympic Winter Games. Thirty-three-year-old pilot Rod Harradence joined a hundred-person, eighteen-aircraft search effort, a dangerous prospect in the storm-plagued area. The search escalated when the Cessna in which Harradence was a passenger went missing four hours after takeoff. Its wreckage, along with three bodies, was found on the slopes of Mount Lougheed. In the continuing search for the original missing plane, a Twin Otter search plane crashed, killing its eight occupants. In all, thirteen people lost their lives. Harradence's serpentine-topped tablet has a white granite core and black granite faces. A photograph on the stone pictures Harradence at the edge of a lake—probably Gull Lake, where he loved to windsurf.

Notes
1. *Calgary News-Telegram*, 20 April 1912.
2. *Calgary Tribune*, 11 November 1885.
3. *Calgary Real Estate News*,
    4 December 1992.

TOUR SEVEN

Sections N and T

1. EGBERT, WILLIAM
1861–1936, 4-2-N

Alberta's third Lieutenant-Governor (1925–31) was born near Welland, Ontario, and served as principal of the Ottawa Normal School before studying medicine at Toronto Medical College. In 1904, Dr. William Egbert moved to Calgary where he set up a medical practice. He was elected alderman in 1909, but lost his bid for the mayoralty in 1910. As one astute observer noted, Egbert "would undoubtedly have been elected had he worked as hard campaigning as did his opponent." Of his defeat, Egbert simply remarked, "I'm just licked, that's all."[1] He served as president of the Alberta Liberal Association (1910–25), the Calgary Board of Trade (1918), and the Alberta Medical Association (1921). In 1935, Dr. Egbert chaired the Economic Safety League, which opposed the new Social Credit party that swept to power that year. Egbert married Eva Miller in 1884. Their son, Justice William Gordon Egbert (1892–1960), served on the trial division of Alberta's Supreme Court from 1950 until his tragic death by drowning a decade later. Justice Egbert's wife, Gladys McKelvie Egbert (1897–1968), was a child musical prodigy and became the first Canadian to win a scholarship to the Royal College of Music in London. Instead of pursuing life on the international concert stage, Gladys returned to Calgary and became an outstanding piano teacher. A grey granite tablet, with the name Egbert carved in relief, marks this family plot.

2. BONE, JOHN
1851–1919, 2-2-N

John Bone's grey granite tombstone is one of the ironies of Union Cemetery. After the city's great fire of November 1886, locally quarried sandstone became the building material of choice, and over the next three decades Calgary earned the moniker "Sandstone City." Over a dozen quarries supplied building stone during the city's pre-World War I boom, including the one operated by Gilbert, Bone, and Oliver. John Bone, a native of Belleville, Ontario, moved to Calgary around 1902 and worked as a stone contractor during the apex of the boom. Partner William Oliver remained in the business until 1915. By 1914, rising labour costs and competition from brick and other materials put an end to Calgary's sandstone era.

3. CHAMBERS, W. J.
1874–1920, 1-4-N

A towering, detailed Celtic cross marks the grave of Dr. W. J. Chambers (1874–1920) and his wife Olive (1887–1977). Dr. Chambers was on his way home from a business trip in New York when he was killed in a disastrous train wreck near North Bay, Ontario. The train had been divided into two sections, each pulled by a separate engine, and Chambers was in the rear coach of the first section. When its locomotive stalled, railway crew from Chambers' train set off explosives to warn the second crew. The roar of the train drowned out the warning blasts, and the second train crashed into Chambers' coach.

Several Calgarians were on board, including Palliser Hotel manager Arthur Bengalia, who lost his right hand as a result of the accident. Dr. Chambers was the only Calgarian among eight passengers who died.

4. WEBSTER, GEORGE H.
1868–1933, 11-6-N

Like his predecessor Thomas Underwood, Calgary's "Cowboy Mayor" hailed from Leicester, England. His family immigrated to Canada in 1873, and Webster grew up in Orangeville, Ontario, and Winnipeg,

A full-sized, white marble figure of a woman in flowing robes, leaning on and gripping a cross, marks the grave of James C. Bentley. The young Bentley family, baby Helena, mother Orlie, and father James, perished one by one in the space of a single year, 1918. (P1)

Manitoba. As Underwood had done, Webster worked on the construction of the CPR, and first passed through Calgary in 1883. He returned in 1900 as the manager of P. Burns and Co., and later made his living in railway construction. Webster became an alderman in 1919 and served as mayor from 1922 to 1926. The Calgary Stampede became an annual event in 1923, and Webster's enthusiastic embrace of western dress, storefront decorations, and other Stampede celebrations set the tone for years to come. By the end of his four-year tenure, Webster had been in office longer than any previous mayor. He was elected to the provincial legislature in 1926, and sat on the opposition bench as Liberal house leader until his death in 1933. His grave is marked by an oval-topped granite tablet.

5. CHRISTIE, NATHANIEL JOHN
1873–1954, 12-7-N

At the end of a fruitless business trip to the west in 1899, hat and fur salesman Nat Christie sat dejected in a Winnipeg hotel lobby, wondering what to tell his bosses in Montreal. Then a tall Alberta cowboy, flush after selling a herd of cattle, walked in and offered to buy drinks all around. Christie was amazed when the man threw down a twenty-dollar bill and told the bartender to keep the change. "I thought if that amount of money was floating about Calgary," Christie later said, "Calgary was the place for me."[2] Christie and his brothers moved west and founded Ontario Laundry, becoming the only laundrymen in Calgary who were not of Chinese origin. He next went into horse raising, becoming president of the Alberta Horse Breeders' Association. Before long he became chairman of the Calgary Exhibition, and from 1926 to 1933—which included the worst years of the Great Depression—Christie served as president of the renamed Calgary Exhibition and Stampede. Though he quit

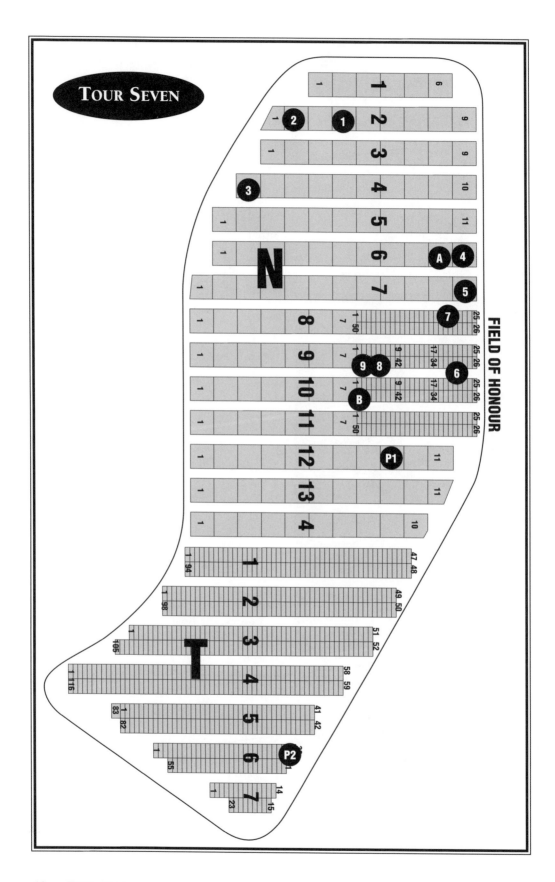

TOUR SEVEN

FIELD OF HONOUR

school at thirteen, Christie helped put his sister Clara through university. Years after her brother's death, Dr. Clara Christie-Might established the charitable Nat Christie Foundation in his memory. A carved white marble headstone marks the Christie family plot, with individual graves marked by white marble foot pillows.

6. FIELD OF HONOUR
(see photo p. 50)

In July 1917, while World War I still raged overseas, the City of Calgary reserved a portion of Section N "for the burial of Returned Soldiers." Over the next seven years, 173 returned veterans were buried in what became Union Cemetery's Field of Honour. Their uniform monuments follow specifications set by the Commonwealth War Graves Commission, and are identical to those found in Commonwealth military cemeteries throughout the world. Inscriptions on the upright tablets include the deceased's rank, name, unit, death date, and age. Some also have individual inscriptions. Symbols include the national emblem or the badge of the veteran's regiment or service, and a religious emblem. In 1923, the Imperial War Graves Commission (as it was originally known) constructed the Cross of Sacrifice, a standard monument of military cemeteries throughout the Commonwealth. That same year, with the exhaustion of available plots imminent, the City of Calgary set aside a second Field of Honour in the new Burnsland Cemetery. A third was later established in Queen's Park Cemetery. As early as 1918, the City had recognized that the Field of Honour at Union would not be sufficient for long, and set aside three blocks in Section S (14–16) for the same purpose. Other Commonwealth war graves can be found throughout the cemetery, where veterans chose to be buried with their families, or in plots they already owned. The last burial in Union's Field of Honour took place May 6, 1924. The City and the Commission entered an agreement that year for the perpetual maintenance of the field. A number of veterans buried there are assumed to have died in Calgary of war-related complications or injuries, but there are some fascinating exceptions, as the stories of HUGH MCSHANE, EDWARD W. PIM, and ROBERT DOUGHERTY MCWILLIAM illustrate.

The Field of Honour was set aside in 1917 and remained in use until 1924. (P2)

7. McShane, Hugh
circa 1893–1923, 20-8-N

Lance Corporal Hugh McShane demonstrated bravery in peace and in war. After returning safely from France, where he served with the 50th Battalion, Irish-born McShane joined the Calgary Fire Brigade in April 1919. He showed particular courage in a 1922 fire, when he continued his rescue efforts even after damaging his own lungs from smoke inhalation. Stationed at Fire Hall No. 3 in Inglewood, McShane was summoned to a prairie fire in east Calgary on October 29, 1923. The fire engine crashed on its way back to the station, and McShane was badly injured. Three weeks later, he died of a blood clot, probably in the lungs. McShane was the first Calgary firefighter to die in the line of duty.

8. Pim, Edward W.
circa 1875–1920, 46-9-N

Thought to be a member of the Pim family of Dublin, which owned one of Ireland's biggest haberdashery firms, E.W. Pim was a "remittance man"—a type well known in early Calgary. Remittance men were the younger sons of well-to-do British families, who gave them a regular stipend as incentive to move to the "colonies." Like many remittance men, Pim enlisted when World War I broke out in 1914. Private Pim served in France with the 31st Battalion, Canadian Expeditionary Force, and returned to Calgary a veteran. On the penultimate day of his life—January 17, 1920—he checked into Room 27 of the Empire Hotel. Pim joined a poker game in the basement that Saturday night, but later returned to his room, and was probably asleep when hotel staff ran through smoke-filled corridors, banging on doors and shouting "Fire!" Most of the two hundred guests survived the blaze that destroyed the Empire and Grand Central hotels, and at first the only casualties were believed to be two men who refused to leave the card game. (See THOMAS W. HUCKVALE.) However, two days after the fire, a block of ice containing Pim's body was discovered in the charred ruins. Pim had apparently made no attempt to escape: he was lying on his back, hands on his chest, his head still resting on what was left of a pillow.

Ten-year-old Frank Percy Langley's grave is marked by a heart-shaped monument that includes small shoes carved in relief, and ivy, symbolizing eternal life. (P2)

9. McWILLIAM, ROBERT DOUGHERTY
1868–1919, 48-9-N

On a cold Monday morning in December 1919, R.D. McWilliam and his son Alex—both postal service employees—boarded the South Calgary streetcar headed for downtown. Hoarfrost made the rails slippery that morning, and as the car picked up speed going down the steep 14th-Street hill, the motor conductor lost control of the car. The difference between life and death now depended on the switch at the bottom of the hill. If it was in the proper position, the car would continue straight north along 14th Street to safety. If someone had opened the 17th Avenue turn-off as a favour to the motorman, disaster awaited. That morning the turn-off switch was open and the speeding car was unable to make the turn. It jumped the track, landed on its side, and smashed into Crooks' Drug Store. The senior McWilliam was killed instantly; his son and a dozen others were injured. Scottish-born McWilliam and his family had moved to Calgary in 1913, just as the pre-World War I boom was about to turn bust. Like so many British emigrés, McWilliam and his two sons enlisted after war broke out. Private R.D. McWilliam served in France for more than two years, suffered shell shock, and was awarded the Military Medal after the battle of Cambrai. His name is misspelled 'McWilliams' on his tombstone.

Notes
1. *Calgary News Telegram,* 13 December 1910.
2. *Calgary Herald,* 4 July 1956.

Section S

1. SANDERS, GILBERT EDWARD
1863–1955, 32-16-S

For most of the years between 1911 and 1932, Calgary's police court was presided over by Colonel Gilbert E. Sanders, a monocled military man whose tough-but-fair sense of justice often took the form of "Not guilty, but don't do it again." Born in Yale, British Columbia, Sanders was educated in Britain and at the Royal Military College in Kingston, Ontario. He joined the NWMP in 1884, and the following year he fought under General Middleton in the Red River Rebellion. During the Boer War (1899–1901), Sanders won distinction as commander of "D" Squadron of the 2nd Canadian Mounted Rifles. He commanded the NWMP in Calgary from 1901 to 1906, and returned to the city in 1911 to become the police magistrate. During his long tenure on the bench (which was interrupted by his service in World War I), Sanders became one of the best known Calgarians of his time. Almost daily, newspapers reported on his judgments. Following his retirement, Sanders became president of the exclusive Ranchmen's Club and of the Calgary Division of the NWMP Veterans' Association. He also served on the Unemployment Relief Commission during the Great Depression. Lead lettering inlaid in his rockshell tablet recalls his career and commemorates his wife Caroline (1859–1938), with whom he is buried.

2. SMART, JAMES "CAPPY"
1865–1939, 26-16-S

In his half-century association with the Calgary Fire Department, including thirty-five years as fire chief (1898–1933), James "Cappy" Smart shepherded its transformation from the volunteer Calgary Hook, Ladder and Bucket Corps into a well-oiled metropolitan force. Born in Arbroath, Scotland, Smart immigrated to Winnipeg where he apprenticed as a mortician. He moved to Calgary in 1884 and

Tree sap has badly stained Frederick Stuart Buchan's Art Deco-influenced monument, a flat-topped, white marble obelisk with a floral pattern in relief. Born in Banffshire, Scotland, Buchan moved to Calgary in 1911 and worked as city treasurer from 1924 until his death in 1940. (P1)

opened Smart and Company, a funeral parlour. In the 1890s Smart served as the fire brigade's hose captain, and delighted in the title because his father, a ship's captain who was lost at sea, had held that rank. Even after his promotion to chief, Smart remained known to all as "Cappy." He led his men from the front lines, risking his life on countless occasions, and suffering frequent fire- and smoke-related injuries. Remembered as a fun-loving, hard-drinking man, Smart played an enormous role in Calgary's social and sporting life. He refereed boxing matches, served annually as grand marshal of the Stampede Parade, and—long before the Calgary Zoo was established—assembled a fire hall menagerie that ranged from bears and parrots to an alligator and a monkey (see LUCILLE MOREY). Smart's moulded concrete tombstone, designed by his personal secretary, George Sweeting, bears a recessed image of his fire hat. The epitaph reads: "His last alarm has sounded."

3. READER, WILLIAM ROLAND
1875–1943, 43-16-S

At nearly the opposite end of the cemetery from Reader Rock Garden lies buried its founder. His unassuming tombstone—a flat marker made from black granite—contrasts sharply with the significance of William R. Reader to Union Cemetery. Born in London, England, Reader studied to become a teacher, but found a career in his first love—gardening. After moving to Calgary in 1908, Reader worked as a landscape planner, wrote gardening articles for the *Calgary Herald*, and helped establish the Calgary Horticultural Society. From 1913 to 1942, Reader served as Calgary's parks superintendent, which included responsibility for designing, developing, and administering Union Cemetery. Reader helped transform Calgary from a relatively treeless prairie town into a city of tree-lined boulevards and diversified public parks, playgrounds, and outdoor leisure and recreational facilities. On the grounds of his official residence at the north end of Union Cemetery, Reader created the nationally acclaimed rock garden that now bears his name. He retired late in 1942 and became manager of the Calgary Ration Board, but died only weeks after assuming his new office.

4. GARDEN, JAMES HAY
1881–1945, (24-25)-15-S

As a city commissioner in June 1915, James H. Garden joined City Engineer George W. Craig for an inspection of the old Centre Street Bridge, which was closed and in danger of collapsing. (Today's bridge, with its stately lion figures, was already under construction.) Without warning, the north span of the old bridge collapsed, sending Garden, Craig, and Edwin Tambling into the swollen waters of the Bow River. Garden was swept downstream and had to be rescued by city employees; Craig managed to grab onto the bridge's timbers and save himself; Tambling drowned. Born in Aberdeen, Scotland, Garden had moved to Calgary around 1905 and established himself as a building contractor. In 1911 he constructed the original Mount Royal College (demolished in 1972) and later served for many years on that institution's Board of Governors. He was elected to three terms as alderman between 1911 and 1924. His monument is a grey granite tablet with a serpentine top.

5. WILLIAM HUMBLE DUDLEY WARD
1877–1946, 21-15-S

Born to a titled English family, Dudley Ward studied at Eton, rowed for Cambridge, and later joined the English Olympic rowing team. Following his family's tradition, he was elected to Parliament while still in his twenties,

Tour Eight

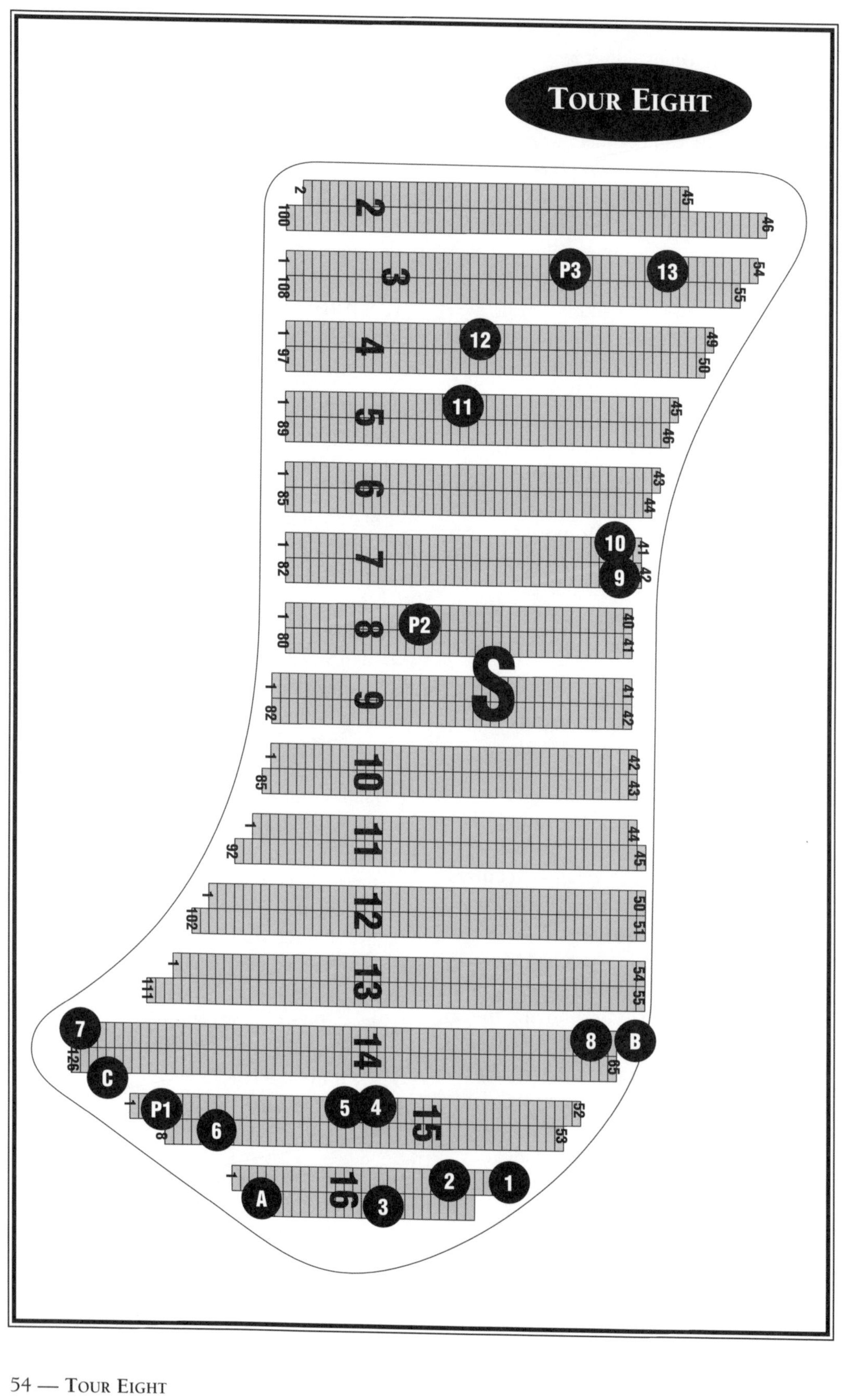
S
2
3
4
5
6
7
8
9
10
11
12
13
14
15
16
P1
P2
P3
A
B
C
1
2
3
4
5
6
7
8
9
10
11
12
13

MAP NOTES

◆ Inexplicably, Section S has no Block 1. Numbering begins with Block 2.

◆ One of the common themes in Section S is the Centre Street Bridge, which was built in 1916 to replace an earlier structure. City Commissioner JAMES H. GARDEN was on the original bridge when part of it collapsed into the Bow River in 1915. JAMES LANGLANDS THOMSON sculpted the artistic elements of the new bridge, including its stately lions. Dominion government architect Leo Dowler (8-3-S) ended his life in 1921 by jumping from the bridge.

NOTES

A. In the 1930s, a second block of mounted police graves at the east end of Section S supplemented the existing block in Section D. Many prominent members of the force are buried here.

B. During Alberta's Prohibition years (1916–24), the mounted police withdrew from Alberta, and its role was filled by the Alberta Provincial Police. Lieutenant-Colonel A. E. C. McDonell ([65-66]-14-S) became its founding commander in 1917. The epitaph on his granite replacement marker outlines McDonell's career, but gives two different spellings of the family name; his wife is identified as Marguerite Caroline Macdonell. Nearby, McDonell's smaller, original tombstone lies flat on the ground.

C. Dr. Arthur Melville Scott, OBE (1869–1941) (124-14-S), served as superintendent of the Calgary School Board from 1905–30, and as superintendent of high schools from 1930–35.

and served as Liberal government whip, Treasurer of His Majesty's household, and Vice-Chamberlain of His Majesty's household. Ward was regarded as a future prime minister, but scandal blotted out his political career. Caught in the open during an air raid alert in 1918, Ward's wife Freda found shelter in a house where a party was taking place. The honoured guest was the Prince of Wales—the future King Edward VIII—who was smitten by Freda. Sometimes called "the first Wallis Simpson," Freda won the prince's affection, but destroyed her husband's career. Ward left her in England and moved to Calgary in 1922, where he oversaw the prince's Canadian investments and established a company called British Industries. Dudley purchased and renamed the Ward Block, which still stands at 105 - 8th Avenue SW. Freda divorced him in 1931, but her relationship with the Prince of Wales ended in 1934.

6. CARR, ALEXANDER (SANDY)
1877–1966, 88-15-S

Born in northern England to Scottish parents, Sandy Carr fought in the Boer War before immigrating to Canada. He settled in Calgary in 1904 and joined the fire brigade, becoming a captain in 1911 and assistant fire chief the following year. In addition to his firefighting activities, which were exciting enough, Carr was at the centre of two dramatic episodes in the city's history. On June 2, 1914, firefighters were summoned to an abandoned warehouse, where police had a murder suspect, Afancy Sokoloff, trapped in the basement. Under Carr's direction, firefighters flooded the basement to force Sokoloff out. Sokoloff pounded on the floor to indicate his position, and Carr chopped a hole to rescue him, disarmed the fugitive, and handed the gun to police. Sokoloff was found guilty and hanged. In April 1929, Carr was part of a recovery effort to find the body of a drowned boy. After setting a dynamite charge to blast through the Bow River's ice cover, Carr and two other men scrambled for cover. Suddenly Carr fell through the ice. With no time to lose—the dynamite was about to go off—retired waterworks superintendent Peter Breen pulled Carr from the water, but fell in himself. The blast went off, and Breen was fatally injured. In 1933 Carr succeeded JAMES "CAPPY" SMART as fire chief, and held the post for a decade. His oval-topped tablet is made of black granite.

7. CAMERON, JOHN MCKINLEY
1878–1943, 1-14-S

A noted defence attorney and one of the best divorce lawyers in Alberta, J. McKinley Cameron was involved in one of the most spectacular capital cases in Alberta's history. In 1922 he defended Emilio Picariello and his associate Florence Lassandro, who were on trial for their lives. Picariello, a bootlegger in the Crowsnest Pass, had made a fortune since the introduction of Prohibition in 1916. After Picariello's son was shot and wounded at a police roadblock, Picariello and Lassandro confronted the Alberta Provincial Police officer, Steve Lawson. A shot was fired, Lawson fell dead, and both Picariello and Lassandro were charged with murder. McKinley Cameron was convinced of their innocence and offered a vigorous defence, but the jury found them guilty and Justice WILLIAM LEGH WALSH issued the mandatory death sentence. Cameron appealed unsuccessfully to the Supreme Court of Canada, and on May 2, 1923, Picariello and Lassandro went to the gallows. The trial became a lightning rod for debate on Prohibition, which was repealed in Alberta in 1924. Cameron was born in Pictou, Nova Scotia, and studied at Dalhousie before moving to boomtown Calgary in 1911. He and wife Ethel (1880–1969) share a black granite

tablet with rolled ends. Their son Stewart Cameron (1912–70) became a well-known editorial cartoonist for the *Calgary Herald*, and worked briefly for Walt Disney Studios.

8. DAVIS, DANIEL "PEACH"
circa 1857–1937, 62-14-S

One of the enduring legends of the NWMP is the tale of the sole Mountie dispatched to meet a U.S. cavalry regiment at the international boundary, and to escort hundreds of Natives from the border to their reserves in what is now Saskatchewan. That Mountie was Constable Daniel "Peach" Davis, so named because of his love of peaches and peach desserts.

Priscilla (Tillie) Cave's original wooden tablet marker was later enclosed in this concrete cast monument, and is visible through a metal-framed glass panel. Born in Manchester, England, Tillie Cave emigrated with her parents in 1913. She died of influenza in 1920 at the age of twenty. (P2)

(The Natives whom he escorted called him "God-Mad-All-The-Time.") Nineteen-year-old Davis joined the NWMP in 1876, saw action in the 1885 North-West Rebellion, and was finally discharged in 1888. During the Mounties' jubilee year in 1923–24, Davis became famous for the tale of his journey with the Natives. By that time Davis was working as a janitor for the City of Calgary. In 1928 the City forced the aging Davis to retire, leaving him and his wife nearly destitute. But "Peach" had not been forgotten. The Imperial Order Daughters of the Empire organized a benefit concert to aid the Davises, emceed by Colonel GILBERT EDWARD SANDERS. Davis' standard military marker bears the NWMP insignia and the force's motto, *Maintien le Droit*.

9. MOLLISON, ANNIE ELIZABETH
died 1929, 44-7-S

Long before the Palliser Hotel opened in 1914, discriminating travellers and long-term guests chose Braemar Lodge, a temperance hotel on 4th Avenue managed by two unmarried sisters, Annie and Jean Mollison. Born in Inverness, Scotland, the Mollisons moved to Canada with their family in the early 1890s. Both sisters went to work for the CPR, managing hotels at Banff, Lake Louise, Field, and North Bend, British Columbia. In 1904 they purchased Braemar Lodge, a residential hotel originally built in 1892 as the residence of Calgary's Anglican bishop. Historian Lewis G. Thomas recalled that "the Misses Mollison managed to maintain an island of gentility more reminiscent of an English spa like Leamington or Sidmouth than of the rakish and rowdy Western hostelry of popular tradition."[1] The wives and daughters of wealthy ranchers stayed at Braemar Lodge, without fear for their reputations or of the drunken men who frequented other city hotels. Known as an excellent pianist, Annie decorated the hotel with the art and antique furniture she collected, and remained manager after Jean moved to Vancouver. Annie died of a heart attack on a Saturday night while conversing with one of the guests in the hotel. Braemar Lodge closed in 1964 and was destroyed by fire while awaiting demolition. Petro-Canada Plaza now occupies the site. Annie is buried in an unmarked grave to the left of Frank Woodward.

10. CRANDELL, EDWARD HENRY
1859–1944, 39-7-S

The former mayor of Brampton, Ontario (1897–98), E.H. Crandell moved to Calgary in 1900 and engaged in a variety of businesses, including the Calgary Pressed Brick and Sandstone Company which he founded in 1905. A company town named Brickburn developed around Crandell's plant west of Calgary, which operated until 1931. Bricks in many Calgary buildings are stamped with the company's 'EHC' mark, and ruins and debris from the plant can still be found in Brickburn, now part of the city and adjacent to Edworthy Park. Before World War I, Crandell contributed land and money to the proposed University of Calgary, whose campus was supposed to be constructed near Brickburn. Crandell proposed subdividing his property as "Varsity Heights," but the university failed and the campus was never built. Crandell served as an alderman from 1914 to 1916, and was president of the Dingman Oil Company. His house later became the residence of wrestling promoter Stu Hart. A red granite tablet with a rare double ogee top marks the Crandell family's grave.

11. THOMSON, JAMES LANGLANDS
1858–1924, 21-5-S

One of the city's few major construction projects during World War I was the Centre Street Bridge, completed in 1916. The design called for ornamental statues,

This black granite cube is unique in Union Cemetery. It marks the grave of Scottish-born engraver William Richards (1844–1920)—a great-grandson of the Earl of Cardonald—and some of his family members. (P3)

and according to lore, Alderman James Hornby was intrigued by a lion sculpture he saw in front of a northwest Calgary residence. The owner, and sculptor, was city labourer James Thomson, a Scottish-born stonemason. Thomson was commissioned to design and construct all of the bridge's artistic elements, including the large city crest and the four concrete lions placed atop the bridge's kiosks, which Thomson patterned after those on Nelson's column in Trafalgar Square, London. Thomson created an original clay model, from which the concrete lions were cast. Brothers Dymtro and William Stogryn, whom the bridge builders called "Cement Joe" and

"Cement Bill," did the finishing work. Thomson probably designed the buffalo heads and floral emblems that adorned the kiosks. The bridge was extensively renovated in 2000, and the lions were replaced by replicas. Thomson also designed Indian heads for the Bow River Bridge in Banff. His blue granite tablet also commemorates his wife and children, including a namesake son who was killed in action in 1916.

12. HUCKVALE, THOMAS W.
1884–1920, 23-4-S

While waiting for their late train out of the city, provincial stock detective Tom Huckvale of Gleichen and his friend, farmer Christie McBride, decided to pass the bitterly cold Saturday night of January 17, 1920, across the street in the Empire Hotel (on the future site of the Glenbow Museum and convention centre). The two friends, along with a handful of other men, got into a poker game in the basement billiard room. According to a later newspaper account, "money was changing hands."[2] The night clerk left his post around 1:30 A.M. and took a hand in the game. Shortly afterward, the hotel porter came down and shouted, "Boys, there's a fire. You'd better get out."[3] Most of the players fled, but Huckvale and McBride had very good hands and stayed behind to play them out. Like them, many of the hotel's two hundred guests did not take the fire seriously, and remained in their rooms. The blaze proved one of the worst in Calgary's history, and several guests had to be rescued at great risk to the firefighters' lives. Huckvale and McBride were found dead of suffocation; the blaze destroyed both the Empire Hotel and its neighbour, the Grand Central Hotel. A red granite western slant marker identifies his grave.

13. MABEE, ALFRED A.
1898–1921, 44-3-S

After World War I ended in 1918, many flying aces became "barnstormers," performing demonstration flights and aerial stunts before hundreds of thrilled spectators. One such pilot was Captain Fred McCall, after whom Calgary's original international airport, McCall Field, was named. To maintain public interest in flying, McCall hired local daredevil Alf Mabee to walk on the wings of his airplane—while the craft was in flight. McCall and Mabee thrilled crowds at the Bowness Flying Field with the "wing-walking" stunt during the 1920 flying season. On June 12, 1921, Mabee performed the stunt several times on the wings of Crossfield pilot Jack Fleming's biplane to entertain a visiting team of Scottish football players. Then Mabee climbed into the front seat and Fleming began the descent to the Bowness aerodrome. But the plane went into a sudden nosedive and crashed near the entrance to Bowness Park. Fleming recovered from his injuries, but Mabee died shortly afterward, making this Calgary's first fatal airplane disaster. The *Albertan* described the Calgary-born Mabee, a car salesman, as "one of the most popular and best-known young men in the city," and as one who "possessed a daredevil spirit and did not know what fear meant."[4] A black granite pillow marker identifies his grave.

Notes

1. Lewis G. Thomas, "The View from Sheep Creek," in *Citymakers: Calgarians After the Frontier* (Calgary: The Historical Society of Alberta, Chinook Country Chapter, 1987), 36.
2. *Calgary Daily Herald*, 21 January 1920.
3. *Ibid*.
4. *Morning Albertan*, 13 June 1921.

TOUR NINE

Sections P, R, and X

1. DINGLEY, DAVID
1880–1920, 65-10-P

2. NICHOLLS, ARTHUR
1883–1920, 67-9-P

No one knows exactly how many city employees have lost their lives in the line of duty. A monument next to the Calgary Municipal Building is dedicated to their memory—but it identifies none of them. Two names that should be there are Arthur Nicholls of the Electric Light Department and David Dingley of the Waterworks Department. Accidents claimed both men's lives during a single week in 1920. At the end of his shift in northeast Calgary on October 31, lineman Nicholls decided to fix a street lamp that might have been broken as a Halloween prank. His colleagues suggested leaving the job until morning. "Tomorrow is my day off and I don't want to leave anything undone," Nicholls replied. "I'll fix that light now."[1] While he was alone, Nicholls accidentally electrocuted himself by touching the live end of the wire. Across town a week later, a waterworks crew set about digging a culvert on 38th Avenue and 14th Street SW. Suddenly, part of the embankment collapsed on labourer Arthur Hollings. Fellow employee David Dingley leapt into the culvert to rescue his friend, but just then the rest of the embankment fell in, killing the would-be rescuer. Hollings emerged uninjured but

Only a few wooden crosses remain in Union Cemetery, and nearly all of them are in Section P. This cross contrasts sharply with Calgary's twenty-first century skyline. (P1)

for a bruised foot. Nicholls and Dingley were buried a short distance apart, within sight of each other's graves. A Bible stands in relief on Nicholls' grey granite monument; Dingley's marker is a black granite tablet with checks in the corner.

3. PILKINGTON, JOHN THOMAS
1873–1934, 88-7-P

Many tombstones in Union Cemetery have an open Bible carved in relief. In John T. Pilkington's case, the Bible says SPIRITUAL-ISM. Pilkington, a native of Lancashire, England, belonged to Calgary First Spiritualist Church, first chartered in 1920 and still active within the city. Members believe that, after death, the immortal soul passes into a spirit world and can be contacted through a medium. Mrs. Ada Gerrard, a clairvoyant medium and one of the founders of the church in Calgary, officiated at Pilkington's funeral.

4. DUNCAN, ARTHUR
circa 1878–1917, 29-7-P

As a twelve-year veteran of the Dumfries-shire police force in his native Scotland, Sandy Duncan earned a reputation as "a fearless man and a remarkably shrewd officer." Duncan and his family resettled in Calgary, where he joined the city police force in 1911, and later became the first of its officers killed in the line of duty. On the night of July 1–2, 1917, he failed to make his hourly call-in and was found dead the next morning behind a vacant downtown building. Duncan had been shot twice, but his own gun was still in its holster. He apparently came upon a gang of thieves who had hidden their loot in the building. "I believe that Arthur came on them quite accidentally, otherwise he would have been prepared," Police Chief Cuddy wrote to Duncan's relatives. "Poor Arthur, they never gave him the least chance to defend himself, but shot him dead in his tracks."[2]

Despite a reward of one thousand dollars, the killer was never identified. Behind Duncan's blunt granite obelisk is a concrete marker that reads "Perpetual care." There are many such markers in Union Cemetery, a relic of the years when city staff cared only for graves that had been sold with a "perpetual care" surcharge. This care was provided free to Duncan's plot, and was eventually extended to all graves in the city.

5. PEERS, THOMAS
circa 1862–1922, 152-5-P

At the turn of the last century, "mixologist" Tom Peers was one of the bartenders at Calgary's finest hotel, the Alberta. ROBERT CHAMBERS EDWARDS, publisher of the *Calgary Eye Opener* was a regular at the Alberta bar. According to historian GRANT MACEWAN, Edwards reckoned that Peers "had dispensed enough liquor to fill every horse trough in Alberta, plus sufficient to float the two ships which made up the Canadian Navy of the day."[3] On one occasion a threatening looking stranger approached the bar, placed his gun on the counter, and pointed it towards the bartender. Peers thought fast. He had been polishing a soda siphon, and continued undistracted—until he had it in position to blast the stranger in the eye. Peers then easily got hold of the pistol. Later, in partnership with another Alberta Hotel barman, Fred Adams (also buried in Union Cemetery, in 6-12-C), Peers bought the Victoria Hotel on 8th Avenue (now the site of the Glenbow Museum). His unmarked grave is two plots to the right of Mildred Moor. To the west, in the distance, the tombstone of Bob Edwards—buried eight months after Peers—is clearly visible.

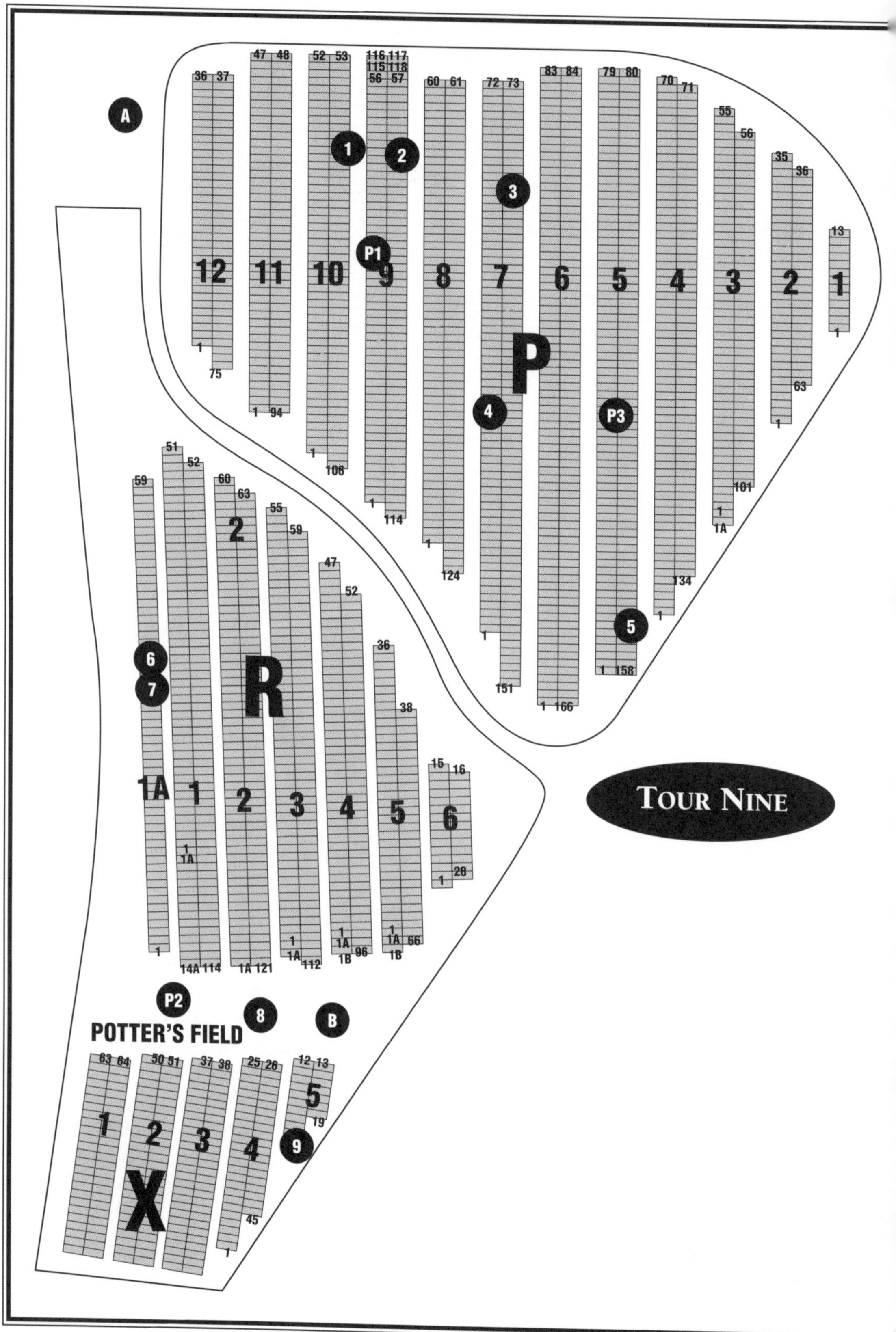

TOUR NINE
P
R
X
POTTER'S FIELD
12
11
10
9
8
7
6
5
4
3
2
1
1A
1
2
3
4
5
6
A
B
P1
P2
P3
1
2
3
4
5
6
7
8
9

6. MILL, WILLIAM
circa 1873–1936, 36-1A-R

The longtime manager of Calgary's National Hotel had ample training in human relations before entering the hotel business. Born around 1873 in Wick, Caithness-shire, Scotland, Mill worked as an Edinburgh police constable and as a warder in a lunatic asylum before immigrating to Canada in 1898. Mill joined the Calgary Police Force in 1906, retiring in 1911 with the rank of Inspector. He took over the King Edward Hotel in 1911, then managed the National from 1916 until his death twenty years later. Mill's tenure at the National included the Prohibition era (1916–24), when the bar remained closed. A black granite tablet names only Mill's wife, Lillian Jesse Mill (1867–1922), with whom he is buried.

7. EDWARDS, ROBERT CHAMBERS
1864–1921, 33-1A-R

Through the pages of the *Calgary Eye Opener*, Bob Edwards' combination of gentle humour, acid wit, and passion for social justice won him a national following, as well as readers in Britain and the United States. Edwards had completed a classical education in his native Scotland and established his first newspaper before his twentieth birthday. After a sojourn in Texas he moved to Alberta, settling in Wetaskiwin by 1897. There he published the first in a series of short-lived small-town weeklies. Before long his sardonic musings on life and politics were reprinted in the *Calgary Herald*, and Edwards' subscriptions soared. By the turn of the century he was judged "the most famous editor of the Territories."[4] In 1902 Edwards launched the *Eye Opener* in High River, moving it to Calgary in 1904. For two decades, Edwards pounded out his one-man journal on a "semi-occasional" basis— that is, when he wasn't on a bender. Eschewing employees, a printing

Only the broad expanse of trimmed grass identifies Potter's Field to the visitor. Here lie some one thousand of Calgary's indigent, unknown, or condemned, all of them in unmarked graves. Public burials took place in Potter's Field until the mid-1920s. (P2)

press, or even a typewriter, the hard-drinking, cigar-smoking editor wrote copy on a rolltop desk in his Cameron Block rooms, now the site of the convention centre. Through satire, bogus "Society Notes" and direct editorial comment, Edwards invested the *Eye Opener*'s every page with his whimsy, literary genius, and social conscience. His reforming zeal eventually led him to politics, and in 1921 Edwards was elected to the Alberta legislature as an independent. He died the following year after making only one speech. Edwards is buried with copies of his publications and a flask full of whisky.

8. POTTER'S FIELD

Near the farthest edge of Union Cemetery lies Potter's Field, the "free burying ground" typical of Victorian graveyards. Its name comes from a New Testament reference (Matthew 27:6-7), in which Judas' thirty shekels of silver were used to buy a field where potters had previously gone for their clay, "to bury strangers in." Here lie the friendless, penniless, and condemned

of Calgary society. An estimated one thousand people were buried here at public expense in multiple, unmarked graves. There are no monuments, and only the broad expanse of trimmed grass identifies Potter's Field to the visitor. Records show many of the burials only by nationality, such as "Chinese man" (1900) and "Russian child" (1905). Interments ended at Potter's Field by the mid-1920s, but public burials in segregated, unmarked graves continued in city cemeteries until the 1970s.

The best-known person buried in Potter's Field is undoubtedly Ernest Cashel (circa 1882–1904). The young fugitive earned headlines late in 1902 when he escaped from Police Chief English, who had arrested him for forging cheques. Cashel lived by his wits for months, during which time he murdered rancher Isaac Rufus Belt. Recaptured in May 1903, Cashel was later charged with murder after Belt's body was found. He was found guilty and sentenced to hang. After a visit from his brother, Cashel produced two loaded revolvers, locked up his guards, and escaped a second time. He was found forty-five days later hiding in a shack seven miles from town. He was hanged on February 2, 1904. The day before his execution, Cashel wrote a letter titled "Advice to young men." He cautioned them to "stay at home, shun novels, bad company and cigarettes."[5]

9. LETHBRIDGE, ROBERT MORTON
1875–1923, 2-5-X

One of Calgary's enduring public institutions stands as a testament to the work of Robert M. Lethbridge. Between 1908 and 1911 Lethbridge supervised construction of the sandstone Calgary Public Library—the first such institution in the province of Alberta—built largely with funds donated by American philanthropist Andrew Carnegie. When a new central library opened downtown in 1963, the original building was designated as the Memorial Park Branch. Lethbridge had fought in a mounted regiment during the Boer War (1899–1902), in which he was injured and invalided home. He left his native England and settled permanently in Calgary by 1906. The son of an architect, Lethbridge became a building inspector for the CPR and later worked for Calgary architects Hodgson and Bates. He served as an inspector of shells during World War I. On June 20, 1923, Lethbridge and contractor Reginald Peach (the father of Calgary historian Jack Peach) were driving towards Midnapore on their way to pick mushrooms. Deep in conversation, the two men did not hear an oncoming passenger train as their truck entered the railway crossing near Turner Siding. The cowcatcher upended their vehicle, injuring both men. Lethbridge died two days after the accident. The doctor who performed Lethbridge's autopsy was Dr. Rosamond Leacock, the sister of humourist Stephen

The tombstone of Sergeant Francis Hall, of the 5th Illinois Cavalry's Company B, is one of many broken monuments that might never be repaired. Cemetery authorities try to contact families if a stone needs repair, but frequently no relatives can be found. (P3)

Leacock. Lethbridge's grey granite tablet has a sunken panel inlaid with lead lettering.

Notes

5. *Morning Albertan*, 1 November 1920.
2. Calgary Police Service archives, letter sent by Calgary Police to relatives of Arthur Duncan, 25 July 1917.
3. Grant MacEwan, *Eye Opener Bob* (Edmonton: The Institute of Applied Art, 1957), 75–6.
4. *Macleod Gazette*, 21 September 1900.
5. Nancy Millar, *Remember Me As You Pass By: Stories from Prairie Graveyards* (Calgary: Deadwood Publishing, 2000), 132.

Sections W and Y

1. HALPIN, CHARLES B.
1864–1955, 21-1-W

Bored with his typesetting job at the *London Free Press* in London, Ontario, nineteen-year-old Halpin came west in 1883 as a CPR construction labourer, and stayed for the next seventy-two years. He became a sergeant in the 90th Winnipeg Rifles during the North-West Rebellion of 1885, fought at the battle of Batoche, and served as one of Louis Riel's guards during the jailed Metis leader's trial. Halpin was present at Riel's execution. He started working for the *Calgary Herald* around 1885 and later edited and published its rival, the *Albertan*. Halpin also worked on newspapers in Banff, Black Diamond, Olds, and Regina. He later published the Lacombe *Western Globe* for thirty years and served as mayor of that town. A simple black granite pillow marks his grave.

2. ALLEN, JOHN LORNE
1878–1946, (38-39)-2-W

Calgary's "Tar and Feathers" case made headlines across Canada in the summer of 1939, and dragged Dr. J. L. Allen's name along with it. Ethel Allen, the anesthetist's wife, was already suspicious of her husband when she discovered an amorous letter to him from nurse Alice Knowles. The doctor and nurse reportedly agreed not to see each other again, and all was forgiven. But when Ethel learned her husband had broken his promise, she evidently had enough. With her daughter Betty in tow,

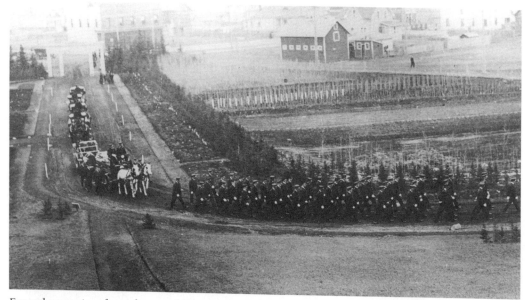

Funeral processions formerly entered Union Cemetery through its neoclassical entrance arch, then followed a tree-lined boulevard uphill to the gravesite. Captain Barney Hodgson's funeral in 1914 began at Fire Headquarters and proceeded to his grave (8-2-L [West]). (Glenbow Archives, NA-2854-42) (P1)

Ethel went to the nurse's downtown apartment and confronted her. According to testimony reported in the press, Ethel held Alice while Betty poured tar over her head. One or both of the women then covered the nurse with feathers from one of her own pillows. After a widely publicized trial, both women were convicted of assault. Betty was sentenced to fifteen days' hard labour and a fine of one hundred dollars; Ethel got forty-five days plus costs. Dr. Allen became a major in the Army Medical Corps during World War II, and later settled in Lethbridge, where he died in 1946. Ethel died in 1969 and was buried near him. Between them lies their daughter, Anne Humphries (1929–71), whose bronze plaque differs only from those of her parents by the bronzed ballet shoes affixed to it.

3. POLLARD, HARRY
1880–1968, 39-3-W

In 1898, seventeen-year-old photographer Harry Pollard left Tillsonburg, Ontario and set up a studio in Calgary. His photographs, and those he acquired from an earlier studio, documented Calgary's development and personalities from its origins in the early 1880s. Many early photographs were lost in a 1914 fire that destroyed Pollard's studio. His photographs of Blackfoot, Sarcee, and Stoney personalities and ceremonies provide a rare early glimpse into Native culture in southern Alberta. He witnessed and photographed the initial discoveries that sparked the 1914 Turner Valley oil boom and its 1947 counterpart at Leduc. In 1924 Pollard became the press photographer for Associated Screen News and the CPR, travelling and photographing the nation and the world. Through his membership in the Canadian Alpine Club, Pollard brought his camera on numerous mountain ascents. In 1911, Pollard married Eleanore Powell (1889–1964), who had been Miss Canada

in 1908. He retired in 1954, and a decade later announced that he would destroy his negatives unless he received fair compensation for their value. The provincial government purchased his collection, which is now housed at the Provincial Archives of Alberta. A granite pillow marker, flanked by two white flower vases, marks the graves of Harry and Eleanore as well as their namesake son and daughter, who both died in 1953.

4. MUNRO, ALEX
1895–1966, 70-3-W

Known as "Mr. Gardener," Alex Munro guided fellow enthusiasts through his weekly *Calgary Herald* column, radio talks, lectures, and personal attention to anyone with a gardening question—but mostly by example as the city's parks superintendent from 1949 to 1960. Munro demonstrated a green thumb while still a schoolboy in his native Ross-shire, Scotland. He apprenticed at nearby Castle Balconie at the age of seventeen, and even grew flowers while serving in France during World War I. He moved to Calgary in 1920, and Parks Superintendent WILLIAM ROLAND READER hired him on the spot. For four decades Munro was at the centre of Calgary's horticultural development. As parks superintendent he oversaw the expansion of parks and recreational facilities into the city's vast new suburban districts. Munro was a president of the Calgary Horticultural Society, and a fellow of the Royal Horticultural Society. An anthology of his writing, *The Calgary Herald Gardening Book*, had sold eighteen thousand copies by the time of his death. He shares a grey granite pillow marker with his wife Rodina.

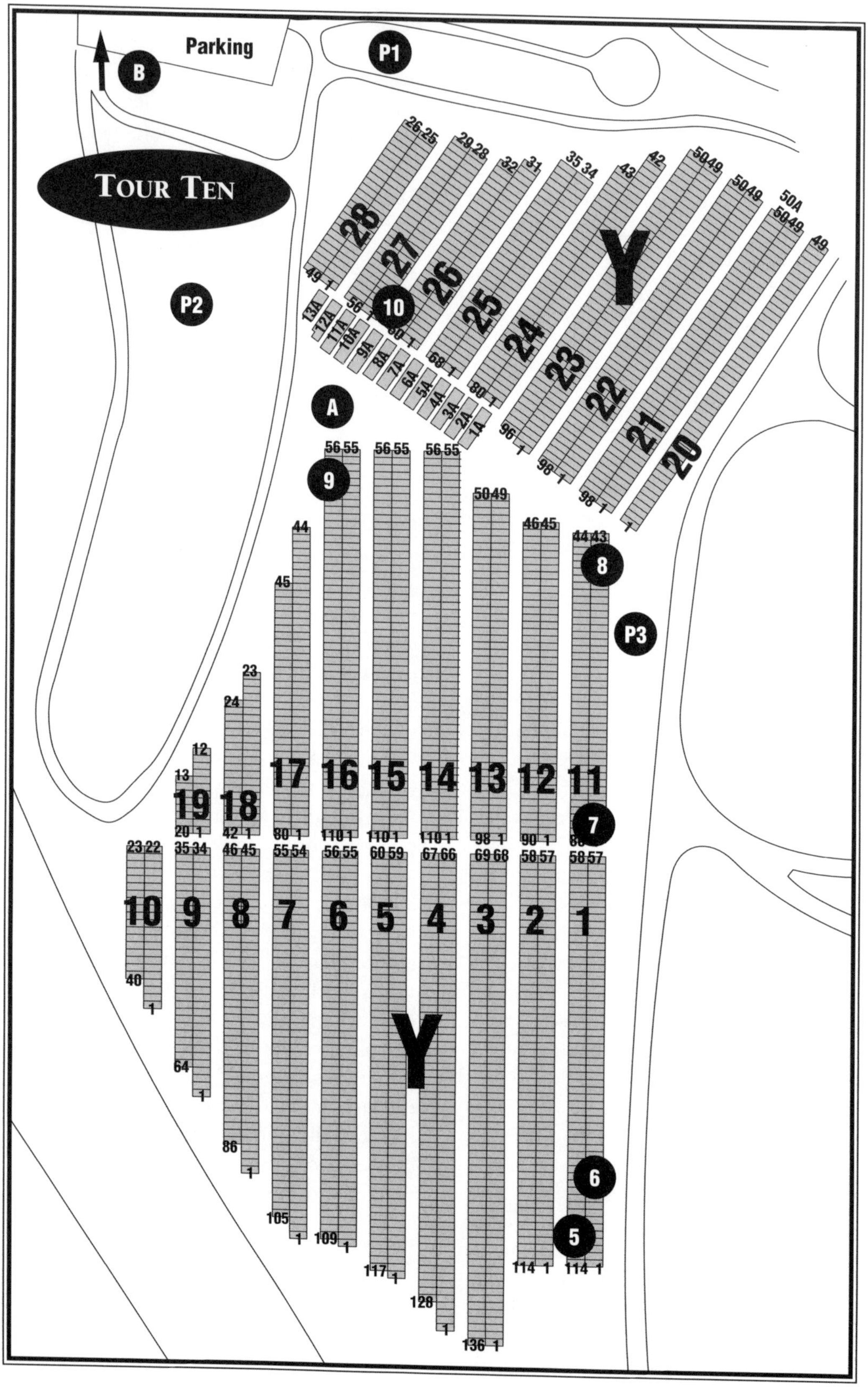
Parking
B
P1
Tour Ten
P2
P3
A
28
27
26
25
24
23
22
21
20
Y
10
9
8
7
6
5
19
18
17
16
15
14
13
12
11
10
9
8
7
6
5
4
3
2
1
Y
13A
12A
11A
10A
9A
8A
7A
6A
5A
4A
3A
2A
1A

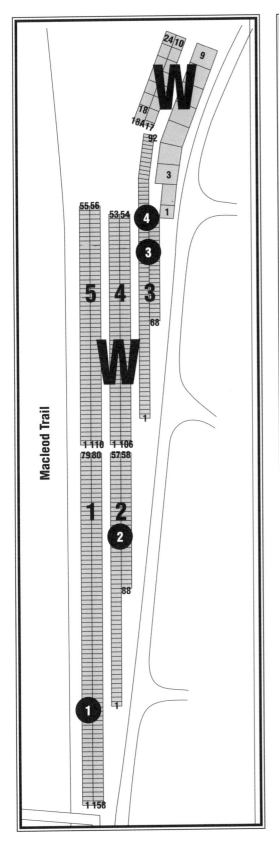

Macleod Trail

MAP NOTES

◆ Burials in the northern area of Section W, which contains family plots, began in 1922. The southern area, comprised of single plots, was first used in 1946.

◆ Flat and pillow markers characterize Section Y, the last to be developed in Union Cemetery. It faces northwest towards Macleod Trail and downtown.

NOTES

A. A scattering ground for ashes is located at the bottom of the hill. Brass plaques affixed to a memorial wall commemorate those whose ashes have been scattered.

B. Just beyond Section Y is the historic entrance arch, built in 1912. After Calgary's Light Rail Transit began service in the early 1980s, the arch was moved to avoid damage from the train's vibrations.

5. ROBINSON, WILLIAM EARLE
1889–1962, 111-1-Y

For nearly a quarter of a century, Bill Robinson presided over Calgary's water supply as the City's waterworks engineer. His years at the head of the Waterworks Department, from 1929 to 1953, were dramatic. The Glenmore dam, reservoir, and water treatment plant were designed and constructed between 1929 and 1933, and the City treated this massive project as a Depression relief effort. Robinson's department operated on a shoestring budget during the Depression, then suffered a manpower shortage during World War II. Robinson shepherded the Waterworks Department through the postwar reconstruction period of the late 1940s and the suburbanization of the early 1950s.

Two columbariums were constructed in the early 1990s for above-ground interment of cremated remains. (P2)

He strongly supported mandatory water meters to reduce excessive consumption, a proposal that has been rejected repeatedly at the ballot box. Robinson's granite pillow marker also commemorates his wife, Helen (1889–1973).

6. MCMAHON, GEORGE L.
1904–1978, 12-1-Y

Calgary's "Mr. Football" came originally from the mining town of Moyie, British Columbia. As a university student in Spokane, Washington, George McMahon played football, earned a business degree, and got to know a young Bing Crosby. Like his more flamboyant brother Frank (1902–86), George earned his wealth in the Alberta oilpatch. The brothers moved to Calgary, and in 1956 both joined the board of the Calgary Stampeders football club. At the time, the Stamps played their home games in the aging Mewata Stadium. George, who served as the team's president from 1960 to 1967, believed that a new stadium was necessary and sketched out a proposal on a cigarette package. The

McMahon brothers put up three hundred thousand dollars—almost one third of the cost—and challenged contractors to complete the facility in 100 days, in time for the 1960–61 playing season. Built on university land, McMahon Stadium was finished 103 days after the sod-turning ceremony. George later served as honorary colonel of the King's Own Calgary Regiment. He is buried among several family members, and a grey granite pillow marker bears the family name. Frank's namesake son, who predeceased him in 1953, is also buried here.

7. FOWLER, JAMES
1887–1959, 2-11-Y

When he retired as principal of the Provincial Institute of Technology and Art in 1952, Dr. James Fowler was one of only two original faculty members remaining from the school's origin in 1916. Popularly known as the "Tech," the institute was established after the failure of the original, short-lived University of Calgary in 1915. (See THOMAS HENRY BLOW.) Born in Hawick, Scotland, Fowler studied at Edinburgh University, and moved to Alberta in 1913 to teach at the Olds School of Agriculture. There he earned six hundred dollars a year less than the school's blacksmith. Within a year Fowler moved to Calgary, where he joined the faculty at Crescent Heights High School under principal William Aberhart, future premier of Alberta. Fowler taught science and mathematics at the Tech from 1916 to 1918, and returned to the institute in 1921 as head of its science department. He became vice-principal in 1929 and principal in 1941. From 1953 until his death, Fowler was the executive secretary of the Community Chest (renamed the United Way in 1973). Fowler's beloved Tech was renamed the Southern Alberta Institute of Technology when a sister institution was established in Edmonton in 1960. A northwest Calgary high school is named for him. A floral relief pattern edges the black granite pillow marker he shares with his wife, Katie Munro (1890–1980).

8. Mackie, James Stuart
1861–1949, 39-11-Y

Though he was born in London, England, Calgary's mayor from 1901 to 1902 was of decidedly Scottish origin. James Mackie immigrated to Canada in 1880, settling first in Winnipeg, where he worked as an agent for J. Hingston Smith & Co., dealers in breech-loading guns. Mackie moved to Calgary in 1886 and founded a fur, gun, and sporting goods store on the future site of the Glenbow Museum. He married Grace MacMillan Forgan in 1892 and became an alderman in 1894, the year Calgary was elevated from town to city status. After six years on council he won the mayoralty, serving as chief magistrate from 1900 to 1901. During his term the City annexed the Exhibition Grounds (today's Stampede Park) and assumed ownership of the facility. Mayor Mackie

played host to the Duke and Duchess of York (the future King George V and Queen Mary) and chaired a committee to create a municipal seal and coat of arms. From 1900 to 1906 Mackie owned a book and stationery store in the Thomson Bros. Block (an historic building incorporated into the convention centre in 2000). He later went into real estate, building the towering Lancaster Building between 1910 and 1919. In 1935, the former mayor and his wife Grace moved into a suite in the Palliser Hotel, where James died in 1949. They spent the evenings of their twilight years in the lobby, reading or visiting with friends. Grace lived in the hotel until 1966 and died four years later, aged 103. A large

Flat and pillow markers characterize Section Y, the last to be developed in Union Cemetery. It faces northwest, towards Macleod Trail and downtown Calgary. (P3)

black granite pillow bears the family name; separate grass markers identify James and Grace. Their grandson Jim became a partner in the landmark law firm of Howard, Mackie in 1957.

9. GREENFIELD, HERBERT
1869–1949, (52-53)-16-Y

A simple black pillow marker belies the significance of Herbert Greenfield, Alberta's fourth premier (1921–25). Born in Winchester, England, Greenfield immigrated to Canada in 1892 and worked as an Ontario farmhand before homesteading near Westlock, Alberta in 1906. He became active in the United Farmers of Alberta, a lobby group that evolved into a political party and defeated the ruling Liberals in the 1921 provincial election. Though he had not run in that election and did not hold a seat in the legislature, Greenfield accepted the premiership and won a seat in a by-election. But he was an inexperienced politician, and resigned after only four years in office. "Herbert Greenfield is neither brilliant nor has he shown particular gifts of statesmanship," wrote a *Montreal Star* reporter in a touching political eulogy. "Yet there is a certain romance about him that has been to some degree responsible for his rise to power and this has been aided by his capacity for hard work, his common sense and his success as a farmer. He is the shining example of the English city boy who came out to Canada to make his fortune and make good."[1] Greenfield was appointed Alberta's agent general in London in 1927, and later served as president of the Oil and Gas Association and the Calgary Board of Trade. He is the only Alberta premier buried in Union Cemetery. Greenfield's first wife, Elizabeth Harris, died while he was premier. In 1926 he married Marjorie Parker Greenwood, who died only months after his passing in 1949. Only Herbert's name appears on their marker.

10. MACEWAN, JOHN WALTER GRANT
1902–2000, 6-27-Y

The flat granite marker he shares with wife Phyllis (1909–90) reads "HUSBAND, FATHER, GRANDFATHER / GREAT GRANDFATHER." It could just as easily have read author, columnist, conservationist, historian, livestock judge, politician, professor, lieutenant-governor, and icon of western Canada. Grant MacEwan's rural Manitoba roots led to his first career as a professor of Animal Husbandry, and eventually, Dean of Agriculture at the University of Manitoba. He moved to Calgary in 1952 as the new head of the Canadian Council of Beef Producers, and served as alderman from 1953 to 1958 and again from 1959 to 1963. MacEwan held a second job as a Liberal MLA from 1955 to 1959, and from 1958 to 1960 he led the Alberta Liberal party. As mayor of Calgary from 1963 to 1965, his first action was to request a cut in salary. MacEwan's populism served him best as Lieutenant-Governor of Alberta, a post he held from 1966 to 1974. He traversed the province by Greyhound bus, demonstrating his common touch and sharing his gentle humour with thousands. MacEwan authored forty-nine books on agriculture, conservation, and history, including a biography of JOHN WARE. Through his boundless energy, enduring charisma, and unshakable personal creed that valued hard work and eschewed waste, MacEwan came to embody the spirit of western Canada that he had popularized through his work. In his final resting-place at Union Cemetery, Grant MacEwan has joined the pantheon of Calgary legends who live on in his writings.

Note

1. Reprinted in the *Calgary Daily Herald*, 30 November 1925.`

KEY TO COMMON SYMBOLS

Anchor: Christian faith, hope (Hebrews 6:19)

Arch: entering into heaven

Bible: piety

Book, open: piety

Column, broken: death

Clover leaf: Trinity

Cross mounted on three steps: Trinity

Crown: reward in heaven

Dove: piety, purity

Finger: pointed downward signifies God reaching to those below; pointed upwards signifies the direction the soul has taken; heaven

Fleur-de-lis: Trinity

Forget-me-nots: remembrance

Gargoyles: overcoming evil, symbolic of Satan

Gate: entering into heaven

Hourglass: passage of time

IHS: Jesus, Latinized contraction of the Greek *IHCOYC*

INRI: *Iesus Nazarenus Rex Iudaeorum*, Latin for 'Jesus of Nazareth, King of the Jews'

Ivy: eternal life, remembrance

Lamb: purity, particularly for children, commonly facing right for boys, left for girls

Lamp: piety

Lily: purity

Stone, draped: death

Sword: victory

Thistle: grief or sorrow

Tree stump: death, signifying a life ended before reaching maturity

Urn, draped: death

Willow: grief or sorrow

FURTHER READING

Blue, John. *Alberta, past and present: historical and biographical*. Chicago: Pioneer Historical, 1924.

Burns & Elliott. *Calgary, Alberta: Her Industries & Resources*. Calgary: Glenbow Alberta Institute [and] McClelland and Stewart West, 1974.

Calgary Public Library, Local History Collection, clipping files.

Dempsey, Hugh A. *Calgary: Spirit of the West*. Calgary: Glenbow and Fifth House Publishers, 1994.

Foran, Max, and Sheilagh Jameson. *Citymakers: Calgarians After the Frontier*. Calgary: The Historical Society of Alberta, Chinook Country Chapter, 1987.

Glenbow Library, clipping files.

Humber, Donna Mae. *What's in a Name...Calgary?* Calgary: City of Calgary Public Information Department and Detselig Enterprises Ltd., 1995.

Knight-Steinbach, Lawrie. *Union Cemetery Interpretive Tour*. Calgary: City of Calgary Heritage Advisory Board, [1994].

MacEwan, Grant. *Calgary Cavalcade from Fort to Fortune*. New ed. Saskatoon: Western Producer Book Service, 1975.

MacRae, Archibald Oswald. *History of the Province of Alberta*. The Western Canada History Co., 1912.

McNeill, Leishman. *Calgary Herald's Tales of the Old Town*. Calgary: Calgary Herald, [1966].

Millar, Nancy. *Remember Me as You Pass By: Stories from Prairie Graveyards*. Calgary: Glenbow, 1994.

Rasporich, Anthony W., and Henry C. Klassen. *Frontier Calgary: town, city and region, 1875-1914*. Calgary: University of Calgary [and] McClelland and Stewart West, 1975.

Trace, Mary Kearns, ed. *Monumental Inscriptions of Union Cemetery*. Calgary: Traces, 1986.

INDEX